T0249301

ONCE OUT OF NATURE

ALSO BY JOY LADIN

POETRY

Impersonation [2022, Revised edition]

Shekhinah Speaks [2022]

The Future Is Trying to Tell Us Something:
New and Selected Poems [2017]

Fireworks in the Graveyard [2017]

Impersonation [2015]

The Definition of Joy [2012]

Coming to Life [2010]

Psalms [2010]

Transmigration [2009]

The Book of Anna [2006]

Alternatives to History [2003]

MEMOIR

Through the Door Life: A Jewish Journey Between Genders [2011]

TRANS THEOLOGY

The Soul of the Stranger:
Reading God and Torah from a Transgender Perspective [2018]

ONCE OUT OF NATURE

SELECTED ESSAYS ON
THE TRANSFORMATION OF GENDER

JOY LADIN

A Karen & Michael Braziller Book
PERSEA BOOKS / NEW YORK

Copyright © 2024 by Joy Ladin

All rights reserved. No part of this publication may be reproduced or transmitted in any form or by any means, electronic or mechanical, including photocopy, audio recording, or any information storage and retrieval system, without prior permission in writing from the publisher. Request for permission or for information should be addressed to the publisher:

PERSEA BOOKS, INC.
90 Broad Street
New York, New York 10004

LIBRARY OF CONGRESS CATALOGING-IN-PUBLICATION DATA
Names: Ladin, Joy, 1961– author.
Title: Once out of nature : selected essays on the transformation of gender / Joy Ladin.
Description: New York : Persea Books, [2024] | "A Karen and Michael Braziller Book." | Includes bibliographical references. | Summary: "Eleven essays on gender written between 2008 and 2021 by one of our leading voices on trans poetics and theology"— Provided by publisher.
Identifiers: LCCN 2024018839 | ISBN 9780892555864 (paperback ; alk. paper) | ISBN 9780892555871 (ebk)
Subjects: LCSH: Gender nonconformity. | Transgender people. | Gender nonconforming people. | Gender identity.
Classification: LCC HQ77.9 .L33 2024 | DDC 306.76—dc23/eng/20240605
LC record available at https://lccn.loc.gov/2024018839

Book design and composition by Rita Skingle
Typeset in Minion
Manufactured in the United States of America.
Printed on acid-free paper.

FOR NANCY AND LIZ,
without whose love and care
neither this book, nor I, would be what we are

and for everyone working
toward generous ways
of talking and thinking about gender

CONTENTS

ACKNOWLEDGMENTS

THIS BOOK HAS BENEFITED from the help, encouragement, and attention of many people, including Nancy Mayer and Liz Denlinger, without whom neither these essays nor this book would be what they are; Trace Peterson, who inspired and published "Trans Poetics Manifesto" and "Diving into the Wreck: Trans and Anti-Trans Feminism," and who has contributed so much to trans poetry and poetics; and Finn Enke, whose friendship and encouragement have deepened my thinking, my heart, and this collection.

I'm also grateful to the editors and publishers of the following essays, in whose publications they originally appeared in somewhat (and sometimes very) different form:

"Confessions of a Born-Bad Mother." In *The Good Mother Myth*. Ed. Avital Norman Nathman. Berkeley, CA: Seal Press, 2014.

"Diving into the Wreck: Trans and Anti-Trans Feminism." *Eoagh*. 9. 2017.

"'Myself—the Term Between': A Trans Poetic Autobiography." (First published as "Girl in a Bottle: an Autobiographical Excursion into the Poetics of Transsexuality.") In *(In)Scribing Gender: International Female Writers and the Creative Process*. Ed. Jen Westmoreland Bouchard. Diversion Press. 2015.

"Ours for the Making: Trans Lit, Trans Poetics." *Lambda Literary Review*. 2.45 (December 6, 2011).

"Supposed Persons: Emily Dickinson and 'I.'" *The Emily Dickinson International Society Bulletin*, 25:1 [May/June 2013].

"Trans Poetics Manifesto." In *Troubling the Line: Trans and Genderqueer Poetry and Poetics*. Ed. TC Tolbert and Tim Trace Peterson. Callicoon, NY: Nightboat Books, 2013.

"What We Talk About When We Talk About 'Gender Dysphoria': An Address to Psychotherapists." (as "Disordering Gender: Breaking the Transgender Taboo.") *Psychology Tomorrow*. 18. 2015.

"Writing Beyond the Human: Divining the Poetics of Divinity." *Poetry*. 216.1 (April 2020).

INTRODUCTION

WHAT DOES IT MEAN to live in a world in which gender is visibly, rapidly changing? How can we understand ourselves and be understood by one another when familiar terms like "man" and "woman" mean different things to different people, and when some people don't identify in familiar terms at all? How do we live, love, and work with those whose identities don't make sense to us, or who identify us in ways that contradict our sense of who and what we are? And how will living among individuals, institutions, and communities who understand and practice gender in different ways change how we talk, write, read, love, relate to our parents, parent our children, make art, pray, socialize, and share a world together?

As Americans reckon with the fact that not all of us identify as simply male or simply female—that there are many people who don't fit the roles and categories offered by traditional, still widely shared binary ideas of gender—more and more of us are confronting questions like these.

Even though, as an openly transgender person, I'm one of the people sparking these questions, I wrestle with them too. Since I began living as myself—living the female gender identification I hid for decades behind a male persona that fit the body I was born into—I have devoted much of my thinking, writing, and speaking to trying to understand how trans and nonbinary identities relate to more traditional ways of doing gender, and to explore how the recognition of these identities is changing gender for everyone. Like many of us, I have been bruised by the often brutal arguments between people who do gender differently from one another; like many of us, I long for alternatives to what those arguments pose as an either/or choice between a world that has no place for anyone who cannot fit binary gender, and a world in which gender has fragmented into a whirl of different beliefs, terms, and ways of life.

I wrote these essays out of a deep desire—really, a lifelong need—to find better ways to think and talk about gender, ways that lead us away from dead-end arguments about whose form of gender is true, or right, or just, or natural, or common sense, or traditional, or progressive, ways that remind us that no matter how others' forms may differ from ours, gender is still and will always be something we do together.

As a trans person living in an often hostile binary world, I understand how hard it can be engage with those whose ideas of gender conflict with our own. It is lonely when those around me don't share my understanding, and painful to relate to those who don't accept my identity. Though we often focus on how individuals identify, even the most individualized forms of gender are inherently social, ways of identifying ourselves and others that, when gender works for us, enable us to feel seen, understood, connected. Accepting that others understand and practice gender differently means accepting that others may not see us as we see ourselves, and that we may not see others, even close family members, as they see themselves. So it isn't surprising that no matter where we fall on the political or cultural spectrum, many of us fear that others' ways of doing gender threaten our communities, our relationships, our very sense of who we are.

Our shared anxieties *could* inspire us think together about how to make the best of a world in which gender is no longer a set of shared assumptions and means different things to different people. But instead, our fears of losing the forms of gender that feel true to us are making it harder and harder to engage respectfully and constructively with those who understand and practice gender in other ways. We hesitate to express curiosity about forms of gender we don't understand, or to explain our own, lest we be criticized or shamed or inadvertently offend by saying something that makes others feel we don't accept their identities. Many of us worry that to listen and speak respectfully to those whose ways of doing gender conflict with our own would tacitly give credence to their views and undermine or betray what is to us the truth about who we and others are.

Each of these essays considers gender from a different perspective, but all aim to reduce the anxieties that drive us apart by thinking and talking about gender in ways that bring us together. Selected from dozens of essays and scores of talks written since my transition in 2007, each offers a different approach to this problem. What they share is the belief that we can understand and live with those who understand and practice gender differently, and that when we do so, we not only learn about others, we learn about ourselves.

At the time of this writing, when assaults on trans and nonbinary people are multiplying, it may seem foolish to focus on fostering understanding across battle-lines and social divisions rather than fighting for the civil rights and basic needs such as health care, employment, and housing on which trans and nonbinary lives, including mine, depend. I wouldn't have been able to do this work if innumerable trans activists, from pioneers such as Miss Major Griffin-Gracy, Kylar Williams Broadus, Victoria Cruz, Marsha P. Johnson, and Sylvia Rivera to contemporary leaders such as Pauline Park, Kiara St. James, and Laverne Cox had not put their lives on the line to make the world livable for trans and nonbinary people like me. Thanks to these efforts, New York City passed groundbreaking human rights legislation banning discrimination on the basis of gender identity and expression, without which my gender transition in 2007 would likely have cost me my teaching position at Orthodox Jewish Yeshiva University.[1] Instead of writing these essays with the status and security of a tenured professor, I, like so many trans and nonbinary people, would have had to struggle to find employment, and might well have not survived at all.

But even as I watch the backlash against trans rights from the relative safety of my white, educated, middle-class blue-state bubble, it seems clear to me that fostering understanding is also an essential form of activism. Trans rights and trans and nonbinary lives will not be secure as long as many non-trans people fear that our identities and rights—our ability to be and live as who we are—come at the cost of theirs, and worry that by being and living as who we are, we threaten the binary forms of gender on which their families, communities, religious traditions, and ways of life depend.

As the anti-trans activists who exploit them know, these fears grow out of widespread lack of understanding of trans and nonbinary identities, and how recognizing these identities may affect binary gender. Anti-trans backlash is also fed by the sense that those who support and accommodate trans and nonbinary people don't understand, and don't want to understand, the anxieties and difficulties that doing so can cause for those who embrace binary gender identities.

The more afraid we are that our ways of understanding and practicing gender, and thus our ways of life, are under attack, the harder it becomes to understand others' ways of doing gender, or to see the common ground, the fundamental human needs for recognition and relationship, that we look to gender to fulfill. The less we understand one another, the more likely we are to treat conflicts between our own and others' forms of gender as existential threats—a vicious circle that makes it harder and harder to recognize and address the needs and anxieties that give rise to these conflicts.

Even apart from anti-trans fearmongering, many non-trans people, including some who identify as lesbian, gay, bisexual, or queer, have profound questions about how recognizing trans and nonbinary identities is changing gender for everyone, and how these changes may affect their ability to identify themselves and others in ways that make sense and feel true to them. That is why relatively minor conflicts between different forms of gender can feel like existential threats to people who aren't involved in or anywhere near them. Whenever our understanding or practice of gender comes out on the losing side of these conflicts, it can feel like we are one step closer to losing our way of being human.

It is not easy to simultaneously live one's gender and try to understand how it seems to those who do gender in ways that conflict with ours. For many non-trans people, accustomed to living in a world that recognizes and reflects their identities, it is hard to think about their ways of doing gender at all, much less to think about them in relation to other ways.

But for most trans and nonbinary people, including me, this kind of thinking is a condition of existence, both before and after we come out to others. In order to hide our gender identities, we have to think constantly about how our sense of who we are differs from how the binary world sees us, what aspects of ourselves we have to betray in order to seem like the boys or girls, men or women, whom others think we are. After we come out as trans or nonbinary, we have to keep thinking about how our ways of living our gender seem from a binary perspective, because in real and sometimes dangerous ways, our lives depend on how non-trans people—family members, co-workers, neighbors, doctors, landlords, bosses, people we meet at parties, people we pass on the street—see us.

Even when survival is not at stake, we often have to consider how our ways of doing gender relate to and may conflict with binary understandings of doing gender in order to do our jobs and interact with our families and communities. For example, when I returned to teaching after my transition, it was immediately clear that my work as a teacher now required me to try to understand how my Orthodox Jewish students saw me, the first openly trans person most of them had ever encountered, and the only faculty member in the university's history who was teaching as a woman after receiving tenure as a man. Some students told me they had been warned away from me by rabbis and parents; some found my gender so disturbing or hard to understand that they struggled to listen to what I said in class; most, sooner or later, tried to ignore my gender (after all, what student wants to spend her time thinking about her professor's gender?) and focus on their studies. I thought about everything I said in class in terms of how it might sound to them, so that I could minimize the obstacles my gender might present to the learning I was there to facilitate, a discipline that forced me to recognize my students' own complex relations to binary gender and the conflicting forms, religious and secular, modern and pre-modern, that they had to navigate in order to live as both Orthodox Jewish and contemporary American women.

It can be disorienting, exhausting, lonely, and sometimes terrifying to think about how my way of doing gender seems to the non-trans people around me, but though this practice grows out of awareness of what divides us, I have found that it can lead to a profound sense of connection, of a shared humanity that is enlarged rather than threatened by our differences.

My classroom experiences have taught me that, despite the conflicts that may arise, people who understand and practice gender in very different ways can work, learn, grow, and live together while remaining true to our sense of who we and others are. That lesson has shaped much of my thought and public work, including scores of essays, a memoir of gender transition, and hundreds of presentations across the country, all aimed at making it easier for non-trans, trans, and nonbinary people to live together.

Though these efforts are forms of trans activism, most of my work has been done on the margins of the trans- and nonbinary-centered activism, scholarship, and community that have flourished in recent decades. I have mostly spoken to audiences that include few trans or nonbinary people; most of my writing has had non-trans publishers; and relatively little of either has been primarily addressed to trans and nonbinary people. Though I was an eager participant in trans-centered conversations and events, particularly literary conversations and events, in the first few years after my transition, over the past decade or so, I have been distanced from them by a progressive disabling illness, ME/CFS, that has increasingly limited my energy, capacity, and activities, and has now left me housebound. As I got sicker, I found I was no longer able to both show up for trans and nonbinary-centered events and respond to the invitations I received from communities struggling to understand trans identities and issues. Forced to choose, I sacrificed connections to trans and nonbinary culture and community that would have enriched both my life and this book in order to devote my waning energies to trying to make it easier for non-trans, trans and nonbinary people to understand and live with one another.

This collection reflects these experiences, choices, and limitations, and, above all, my belief that people who do gender in different ways can and need to understand one another, and that doing so can lead all of us to creative, psychological, and spiritual perspectives beyond those afforded by our own forms of gender.

The essays in Section I, "Trans and Other Ways of Being Human," grew out of my efforts to explain transgender and nonbinary identities and lives to non-trans people accustomed to thinking in terms of binary gender and seeing gender as determined by or indistinguishable from physical sex. Rather than focusing on differences between those who do and those who don't fit binary gender, these essays work to show how transgender and nonbinary lives grow out of, and can help us understand, the common challenges of being human: the mismatch between our sense of who we are and bodies that keep changing and never fully express who we know ourselves to be ("Once Out of Nature"); the strain of not fitting social roles and categories ("What We Talk About When We Talk About Gender Dysphoria"); and the experience of being seen, and seeing ourselves, as Other ("We Pass for What We Are").

Section II, "Trans and Other Women," turns from how we can understand ways of doing gender that seem foreign to us to an even more difficult question: how we can respond to and learn from conflicts between our own way of doing gender and ways that seems to threaten it. Drawing on my own experiences, these essays focus on one of the oldest and bitterest of these conflicts: whether people like me, born and raised male but identifying and living as female, should be accepted as women. The first essay, "Confessions of a Born-Bad Mother," discusses how I was seen as a parent before and after my gender transition. The second essay, "I am She as You are She as You are Me and We are All Together," moves to the social media arena, using online criticism I received in response to my transition to examine battles over the meaning of the word "woman": what it means when others reject or alter the basic terms of our identity; whether there can be common ground among those who define "woman" in conflicting ways; and what such conflicts can teach us about the nature of gender. The third essay, "Diving into the Wreck," explores whether conflicting ideas of gender are mutually exclusive by considering the decades-long battle between trans and anti-trans feminists over whether feminism should consider people like me to be women. The essay compares trans and anti-trans feminist ideas of gender, looks at how each idea has shaped the other, considers the consequences of each, and uses Adrienne Rich's famous poem, from which the title is taken, to imagine a feminism that embraces both despite their contradictions.

Rather than trying to foster understanding and find common ground between those who do gender in different ways, the essays in the final section, "Trans and Other Acts of Self-Creation," explore the creative potential of living in a world in which, because there is no universal idea or language of gender, there is no universally accepted way to conceive and express who we are. The first essay, "Ours for the Making," written when the idea of "trans literature" was still in its infancy, proposes a trans literature which, unlike women's or gay and lesbian literature, is not defined in terms of the identities of writers but by its trans poetic ambitions to create language for ways of being human for which language does not yet exist. The brief second essay, "Trans Poetics Manifesto," expands on the idea of trans poetics and invites writers of all gender identifications to engage in it. The third essay, "Supposed Persons," zeroes in on specific efforts to use language to express unconventional ways of being human, comparing my personal difficulties in saying "I" as a person who doesn't fit binary gender assumptions with the complicated, often subversive ways in which the famously unconventional Emily Dickinson makes the pronoun "I" mean what she wants it to mean in her poems and letters. The fourth essay, "Myself—the Term Between," extends trans poetics beyond literary texts to include the problems of living and writing about ways of being human that don't fit conventional categories by examining how my efforts to express my trans identity in my life and poetry shaped one another. In the final essay, "Writing Beyond the Human," I push trans poetics even further, explaining how it helped me write poems that, rather than a human "I," express the "I" of the Shekhinah, Jewish mysticism's name for the immanent, female aspect of God, whose perspective, self, and way of being are, as the title of the essay suggests, beyond the human.

Taken together, these essays try to show that rather than focusing on our fears and rages, we can think and talk about gender in ways that not only help us understand and live with one another, but teach us about things that are ultimately more interesting and important than gender: how we can live authentically as individuals and in productive, compassionate relation to others; how to recognize the humanity of those who don't fit our assumptions about what it means to be human; what we have in common with those we see, and those who see us, as fundamentally different; and how our lives, individually and together, illuminate the mysteries of being human and the mystery beyond us.

A NOTE ON TERMINOLOGY

FOR MANY OF US, particularly older people like me, one of the most anxiety-producing aspects of the way gender is changing is the loss of a shared language that, however well or poorly it fit us, we could count on others using and understanding. Even those of us who are happy to live in a world in which there are ever more languages of gender know how hard it can be to relate to people who use a language of gender that seems foreign or wrong to us, or who use what seems like our language of gender in ways we don't expect, approve, or understand, or who refer to us ways that make us feel misunderstood, misrepresented, disrespected, or erased.

These essays try to use language in ways that avoid exacerbating these problems, and to offer language that includes those who do gender in different, sometimes mutually unintelligible, ways. But since we have barely begun to develop a common language in which we can talk about our different ways of doing gender, I know that my language won't work for or make sense or feel respectful to everyone. One way I know my language falls short is my inconsistency in acknowledging people who identify as "nonbinary," a term which, as far as I know, has no fixed definition, but which I take as meaning that, for those who identify this way, available terms for gender identification do not work and shouldn't be applied. I apologize for those failures, and any hurt they cause. I meant, and mean, to do better.

When I was very young, I thought there was no word for what I would now call my way of doing gender. And while I'm grateful that there are now many words for people like me who don't fit binary gender definitions, none of those words captures all the facets of my relations to gender, and, because new words keep appearing, I'm never sure others will share or understand the terms in which I identify myself.

In the hopes of making myself clear, these essays refer to my sense of and relation to gender in a number of different ways, some of which are widely known, and some of which I have developed myself. When I refer to the sense of who I am that has persisted since earliest childhood, I talk about my "female gender identification," a cumbersome term intended to get away from the fraught question of what gender I really, essentially am—a flashpoint in many conflicts between different ways of doing gender—and focus instead on who I feel and know myself to be. When I refer to my particular form of transgender identity, I use the first, and for much of my life only, term I knew for my relation to gender, the now old-fashioned (and for younger people, excruciatingly uncool) "male-to-female transsexual," a diagnosis developed by doctors to justify medical treatment of patients tormented by the sense that we really, essentially, *are* the gender opposite to our physical sex.

I also identify myself in ways that connect me more broadly with others who don't fit binary gender definitions, such as "transgender" or "trans," or, as I did above, "people like me who don't fit binary gender terms," terms intended to embrace not only transsexuals but people who embrace many other relations to gender and identity, including those who identify as nonbinary. When I identify myself as "transgender" or "trans," I am associating myself specifically with those who not only don't fit binary gender terms but for whom moving or living between gender categories is central to their lives and sense of who they are.

While I use binary gender terms, like "male" and "female," in their conventional sense, I don't refer to people who identify in binary terms as "cisgender," a word generally used to mean being the opposite of transgender, i.e, being someone who completely fits his or her assigned gender. Since I don't believe it is possible for anyone to completely fit any gender categories, to me, "cisgender" seems like a reductive characterization that flattens and erases individuality, reinforces essentializing binary thinking, and deepens social divisions by implying the absolute difference between those who do and those who don't fit binary gender. Instead, I refer to people who are neither transgender or nonbinary as "non-trans," a term that names what they aren't rather than presuming to define what they are.

In keeping with my goal of finding language that fosters under-standing among those who do gender in different ways, I avoid pejo-rative terms for those who embrace systems of gender that have no place for people who identify as transgender or nonbinary, referring instead to "gender conservatives," "gender traditionalists," or "people who embrace or defend binary gender." I sometimes distinguish reli-gious defenders of binary gender, who see maleness and femaleness as divinely decreed and assigned by God, from secular defenders, such as feminists who are critical of the idea of gender that is not rooted in physical sex. When talking about feminists who defend binary gender systems, I avoid pejoratives such as "TERF" and use the term "anti-trans feminists," not because I want to suggest that their feminism con-sists of nothing more than opposition to recognizing transgender and nonbinary identities, or that they are all the same (they are not), but to highlight what, in the context of these essays, is their shared defining characteristic.

To me, the most important term in these essays is "we," a term in which, unless otherwise qualified, I mean to include everyone, regardless of how we identify ourselves or what way of doing gender we embrace. Anxieties about gender and the acrimonious battles that grow out of and feed them to have made it harder and harder to say "we," harder and harder to recognize or even imagine the common human ground that underlies our different ways of doing gender. I mean these essays to reinvigorate our sense of "we" when it comes to gender, to encourage us to say "we" in ways that embrace conflicting forms of gender and remind us that however many forms it takes, gen-der is always something we do, and must learn to do, together.

ONCE OUT OF NATURE

I

TRANS AND OTHER WAYS OF BEING HUMAN

Once Out of Nature:
Reflections on Body, Soul, Gender and God
(2013)

> Once out of nature I shall never take
> My bodily form from any natural thing,
> But such a form as Grecian goldsmiths make
> Of hammered gold and gold enamelling . . .
> From W.B. Yeats, "Sailing to Byzantium"

ONE SUMMER, I promised myself that I wouldn't miss a sunset. I would set out on foot along my suburban street, toward the blaze of molten gold limning our small local mountain. I wasn't far from farmland. Half a mile away, a little-used dirt road threaded fenced-off pastures of profoundly uninterested cows. If I walked far enough, on the right hand side I'd come to a grass-fringed mudhole dug to water cattle, and, if I was lucky, glimpse a great blue heron or thrumming bullfrog.

This was nature, I would think, real nature, whose wings still beat in the mountain's lengthening shadow.

But was it? The herons were only here on account of the mudhole, and the mudhole was dug out to give domesticated cattle access to water. My decision to label part of the scene "real nature" was a romantic simplification, a projection of human categories onto the unsubdivided sprawl of life.

There's nothing natural about our notions of nature. "Nature" is a human category, a construct that reflects our longing to define our place in the universe we simultaneously inhabit and conceive. During my open-mouthed awe at the startled herons' flight, "nature" meant an order human beings may witness, protect or despoil, but necessarily stand outside, because "nature" is defined in opposition to us. But the idea of "nature" also grounds our conceptions of humanity. People seem natural to us when they reflect what we oxymoronically call "human nature"—our sense of how people are and should be.

The artificiality of ideas of nature and human nature is old news to philosophers, anthropologists, psychologists and others who study human minds and culture. But what's old news in academia is still a matter of life and death to people like me—people whose gender doesn't fit the "natural" binary categories of male and female. Those who see transgender and nonbinary people as "unnatural" have a tendency to ostracize us, fire us, evict us, assault us, and, particularly if we are people of color, murder us. I've been lucky. Over my fifty-plus years, the worst harm I've suffered comes from self-inflicted wounds. Like many trans kids, I grew up tormented by my inability to understand myself in terms of "natural" categories of male and female. The combination of my male body and my unshakable sense of being female seemed, and still seems, to exile me from human and any other kind of nature. Even now, after years of living as a woman, my gender doesn't feel natural to me.

My gender is a mudhole, a willful remixing of physical and human nature that defies separation into neat categories like male and female, natural and artificial, challenging the idea that those categories are mutually exclusive, that we can clearly, conclusively, distinguish them at all. That, perhaps, is why some react so violently to people like me. We are mirrors in which they see the artificiality of the "natural" binary of male and female, its incompleteness, its inadequacy, the contradictions it simplifies.

I understand that anger. I spent most of my life longing to be, as the song says, a natural woman. But the longer I live as my true self—as a woman whose every female X chromosome is invariably paired with a Y, and who was born and bred male—the happier I am to live outside of nature. I am what I am and I do what I do without fretting about how I fit or conflict with "natural" ideas about what a woman should be or do. It can be cold and dangerous outside the gender binary, but you can't beat the view of the gloriously messy category-confounding universe.

But you don't have to be transgender to experience a destabilizing dissonance between the bodies we are told naturally define us, and the sense of self we refer to whenever we say "I." We see this when the aging speaker of Yeats's "Sailing to Byzantium" declares, "Once out of nature, I shall never take / my bodily form from any natural thing." Like me, Yeats's speaker is dismayed by the mismatch between body (Yeats's speaker calls his "a tattered coat upon a stick") and soul. But

Yeats's speaker goes much further than I have, rejecting not only his "bodily form" but "nature" itself. In what someone somewhere has no doubt already identified as an early example of post-humanism, the speaker tells us he looks forward to spending eternity in "such a form as Grecian goldsmiths make / Of hammered gold and gold enamelling." Becoming "artifice" rather than "natural thing," he believes, will enable him to sing of "what is past, or passing, or to come" without having to suffer through it.

Like Yeats's speaker, I looked forward to dying, to shedding the body that was doing such a bad job of housing my soul. Like many trans children, I occasionally tried to kill my body to escape the pain it gave me; unlike all too many trans kids, I wasn't good at suicide, and my body and I continued hurting and being hurt by one another into my mid-forties.

Unlike Yeats's speaker, my longing for death was driven by despair rather than hope. I didn't want to escape nature—I wanted to fit into it, to have a body that would fit my female gender identity. If I couldn't live in a body that felt like mine, I didn't want to live. Around the age of eight, I discovered my first glimmer of hope that I could find my way into nature. One of my mother's magazines included a poignant maternal tale of a son's transformation into a daughter. Apparently, I wasn't the only one of my kind. In addition to males and females, humanity included people like me, "transsexuals."[2]

I knew that being transsexual wasn't the same as being male or female; nothing I'd ever heard about nature or human nature included people who were born as one sex but felt they truly were the other. For the mother in the magazine, as for many, not fitting into the gender binary was a medical problem, and she and her child were grateful for the medical process, called "sex change" then and "gender reassignment" now, through which transsexuals could take what felt to us like our natural places in the gendered world.

Most non-trans people think of gender reassignment only in terms of genital surgery. But gender reassignment isn't genital reassignment. Few people express our own gender or recognize others' by comparing genitalia. Sex is physical, biological. Gender, as many have noted, is a language, an arbitrary collocation of public signs, such as hair length or handshake firmness, we use to express both shared and personal meanings. Like other languages, gender is mutable, negotiable, historically and culturally contingent, a shifting collocation of individual idiom and long-established convention, a medium of public expression, and a means of understanding and expressing ourselves.

Gender reassignment isn't a medical intervention; it is the syntax by which the language of gender enables those who feel wrongly "assigned" to male or female identities to unfold and express who we know ourselves to be.

From the outside, gender reassignment can seem artificial, superficial, a silly insistence that the trivial nouns and verbs of gender—suits and skirts, tones of voice, arcs of arm and swings of hip and, God help us, makeup—have existential importance. But Yeats considered artifice the ultimate expression of self (in "Sailing to Byzantium," artifice is one of eternity's main selling points), and when I began the gender reassignment process, I realized how stunted my artifice-starved female gender identity was. My male persona was just that, a persona, a conscious attempt, driven by fear and shame, to look and act the way others wanted me to. Everything, from my personal taste to my morality, was a mask, a pretense, a way of hiding who I really was. As a result, when I began living my female gender identification full-time—when I began living as a woman—I couldn't answer basic questions about who I was, because I had spent my life avoiding them. Was I the kind of woman who wears scarves? Climbs mountains? Belly dances? Runs for public office? I didn't know. Like anyone learning a new language, I needed to master the basic nouns, verbs and syntax of femininity, to learn how to dress, talk, move through the world as a woman, before I could attempt any grander statement about who I was or wanted to be.

The artifice of gender reassignment, the changes in my physical appearance and social presentation, enabled me, after 40-plus years, to finally see myself in the mirror. But gender reassignment also enabled me to step outside the mirror, to walk away from the compulsive, self-defeating cycles of introspection through which I, like so many trans people, kept trying to determine whether my sense of gender identity was real, was true, was indeed my identity and not, as most of the world insisted, delusion, impossibility, sexual fetish or mental illness. The artifice that identified me to others as a woman was to me a crucial expression of selfhood, a means of embodying and making visible my disembodied, invisible identity. It enabled me to speak as myself, write as myself, teach as myself, care for my children as myself, make friends as myself, suffer, endure, and love as myself.

The artifice that enabled me to walk the world as a woman helped me to recognize my body as mine, to feel at home within my skin—to feel. When I lived as a male, I worked hard not to feel. Awareness of my body made me feel sick, entombed, buried alive in a not-me that was supposed to be me. Gender reassignment changed all that. Suddenly, I felt connected to my body—I realized that I *was* my body—and between the thrill of physical existence and the elevation of my estrogen level, I found myself awash in feeling. But having had so little emotional experience, I had no natural responses to feelings. I almost never cried when I was a man. Should I cry now, and if so, when? When I was in pain? When I was sad? afraid? happy? When I met a friend, should I hug at the beginning of our interaction? at the end? What were the right ways to express feelings, the ways "natural" women expressed feelings, the ways I would express my feelings if I had grown up female?

I knew those were silly questions. I knew that everyone grows into our own versions of human nature through a combination of social-ization that teaches us how people "naturally" are, experimentation through which we discover how to adapt those inherited notions to our own needs and situations, and habitual repetition that makes what we do seem natural to ourselves and others. But I had spent my life longing to take my place among "natural" females; now that I was finally becoming my true self, I found myself in a world of people who doubted, sometimes violently, the claim that someone like me had a place among the naturally male and female. Those skeptics took very seriously the same silly questions that kept me up at night: when I spoke as a woman, dressed as a woman, presented myself as a woman, was I doing the right things, the things natural women would do, things that would qualify me to take my place on the female side of the gender binary, or was I, as the feminist scholar Germaine Greer has called people like me, "a ghastly parody of women"?[3]

I don't know how Yeats would have felt about gender reassignment, but he might have felt some satisfaction in gender reassignment's demonstration of the fact that human beings create and reveal ourselves through artifice. Intellectually and practically, I agree with Yeats; it's silly to fret about whether what I do qualifies me as a real woman, and such anxieties tend to reinforce narrow, damaging stereotypes of what women are and can be. But I am still saddened by the knowledge that my identity, like all human identity, is not the revelation of some "natural" self but an act of self-fashioning, choice, artifice, imagination. I grew up imagining that others, unlike me, really were the boys and girls, men and women they appeared to be, that their identities weren't identities at all but natural, unchanging essences. I spent my early years in a silent argument with Pinocchio, sympathizing with his desire to be real but unable to understand why he wanted to be a real *boy*.

And so it came as a shock to me to discover, when I began the gender transition process, that identity was so mutable that I could refashion mine in a matter of minutes. Because my height is within female norms, long before I had embarked on the medical aspect of gender reassignment, I could walk into a single-stall bathroom as one gender and emerge minutes later as the other. For a couple of years, I commuted back and forth across the gender binary, sometimes several times a day. It was magical, but spooky. All my life, I had thought of gender as a natural law, to be circumvented only through divine or arduous medical intervention. Now, I saw that both the male persona within which I felt imprisoned and the female "true self" I had longed to become could fit in the same shoulder bag.

Many transgender people happily express their gender identities via this sort of manipulation of the language and artifice of gender. But transsexuals are defined by our need to not only reshape our public gender identities but the "bodily forms" in which we live, because those bodies don't feel like ours. Transsexual writings are strewn with attempts to describe this painful, disorienting, often life-destroying disjunction between body and soul. Therapists say we are experiencing "gender dysphoria." We say we haunt our bodies (when I played with my children as a man, I saw myself as a paternal version of Casper the Friendly Ghost), or that we feel like the living dead, that our bodies feel as numb as diving suits, as flat as cardboard cutouts. We can't stop feeling our estrangement from our bodies, can't stop yearning for bodies that fit our gender identities, imaginary bodies that seem as real and tragically out of reach to us as amputees' phantom limbs.

There haven't been many scientific studies of the neurobiology of transsexuals, but phantom limb syndrome may suggest a physiological basis for our conviction that we are living in the "wrong" bodies. Human brains constantly map our bodies, distinguishing self from not-self, coordinating relationships between senses, limbs and the world around us. Transsexuals' sense that our bodies are "wrong" may, like amputees' sense that amputated limbs are itching, reflect the attempts of brains to map male or female bodies that aren't there.

It's comforting for me to think that there is a "natural" explanation for my "unnatural" gender identity, but even if a brain scan showed that my brain fits male norms, my sense of who I am would remain. And whatever the cause, transsexuals' sense of gender identity is so profoundly at odds with the sex of our bodies that we endure enormous costs—physical pain, social exile, loss of family, home, profession—in order to make those bodies, and the lives we live through them, better reflect our souls.

For many, that's what seems most unnatural about gender transition—our insistence on altering healthy bodies in response to feelings non-transsexuals can't imagine. Of course, many of the ways transsexuals alter our bodies during transition *are* "natural," that is, practices common among human beings, who in every time or place seem driven to refashion our bodily forms by shaving, trimming, clothing, coloring, scenting, and otherwise physically modifying ourselves to reflect personal preferences and social norms. I did a lot of shaving during transition, but so do many "natural" women and men. I got my ears pierced, I bought new and very different clothes, I started wearing makeup. Such behaviors might seem unnatural because they violate social norms for male gender expression. But as I've learned during fifty-odd years in which it's become common for women to wear jeans and men to wear earrings, it's natural for the social norms we dub "human nature" to change.

Ear piercing is common among both men and women these days, though only transsexuals seek medical interventions to relocate ourselves from one side of the gender binary to the other. None of those interventions are natural—this is Western medicine we are talking about—but the most important, "hormonal replacement therapy" or "HRT," in which transsexuals are given hormones of the opposite sex, actually prompts our bodies to change themselves. Most "secondary sex characteristics," the physical traits that lead us to identify someone as male or female—presence or absence of breasts, proportion and distribution of fat and muscle, type and distribution of hair—are responses to the ratio of androgens to estrogens. Most human bodies produce both estrogens and androgens. Unless we are intersex, when estrogens predominate, our bodies respond by expressing traits associated with female bodies; when androgens predominate, our bodies respond by expressing male characteristics.

HRT isn't only, or even primarily, for transsexuals. Many genetically female women undergo HRT, taking artificial estrogens and progesterones for menopause, birth control and other situations that have nothing to do with gender reassignment. Genetically male men undergo HRT too, taking testosterone for conditions ranging from prostate cancer to sexual dysfunction.

But as the term "hormone replacement therapy" suggests, for nontrans people, HRT is designed to "replace" what doctors have determined is the natural, normal, or healthy level of sex hormones. For transsexuals, the purpose of HRT is to shift our bodies' natural ratio of hormones to ratios associated with the opposite sex.

The result of this shift is a natural process: adolescence. For most of us, adolescence refers to the one-time process of transforming children's bodies into the bodies of men and women. For transsexuals, HRT prompts a second adolescence. As my endocrinologist's treatments decreased my testosterone level below male norms and increased my estrogen level to female norms, my body naturally responded by growing breasts, moving fat cells from my cheeks and stomach to my hips and buttocks, thinning my body hair, softening my skin, slowing my metabolism, and otherwise acting like a female body. Had I undergone hormone replacement treatment before my testosterone levels began to rise when I was thirteen, apart from my chromosomes, internal organs and genitalia, I would be physically indistinguishable from any "natural" woman. But it isn't natural to go through a second adolescence, and some of the changes of my first can't be undone: neither my voice, my bone composition and skeletal structure, nor my voicebox, were changed by HRT.

Though the results of my medically-induced second adolescence fall short of a natural female body, I thank God every day I wake up and my sleepy brain finds itself in a body that feels like mine.

According to the trans/cis binary promoted by trans activists as an alternative to the traditional male/female binary, there are two kinds of people in this world: people who fit binary categories (male and female, natural and unnatural, and so on), and people like me, who don't. Actually, though the gender binary's defenders and trans activists might argue with me, I don't believe there are any people who perfectly, constantly, essentially fit binary categories. We are too complicated, and binary categories are too simple. But it's human nature to sort non-binary phenomena into binary categories; it's natural for human cultures to ensconce binaries as the cornerstones of worldviews and values systems; and it's natural for human psyches to cling to and defend binary categories when confronted with people like me who confound them.

But however natural those we are accustomed to may seem, binary categories are as artificial as the binary ones and zeroes of computer languages. If you look hard enough at any aspect of nature, you will find things that defy the either/ors of binary classification. The binary categories of "life" and "non-life" seem to cover all the possibilities, but virologists and EMTs trying to revive heart attack victims can testify to the crowded murk between them. The interminable American debate over abortion demonstrates how desperate we are, and how futile it can be, to try to reduce humanity to binary categories like fetus and person.

Given the human propensity for binary thinking, it's natural that many people aren't sure what to do with folks like me: which pronouns to use (common courtesy dictates using the pronouns we prefer, but things get more complicated when it comes to identifying us as mothers or fathers, sons or daughters, sisters or brothers, or even referring to past and present versions of us), and whether to admit us into same-sex groups or spaces. (Bathrooms, locker rooms, public showers, dormitories, prisons, same-sex colleges, women-only events, rape-crisis hotlines and shelters, gender-limited religious roles like Catholic priest, and sports competitions provoke some of the strongest disputes.)

Some find trans people so unnatural that they deny our very existence, arguing that trans identities aren't identities at all, but sexual fetishes, symptoms of mental illness, or attention-getting stunts. Some say that that our existence is an affront to God, society, morality, and the natural (binary) order on which everything, they believe, depends. Many Americans still believe that it is natural to deny us employment, housing, health care (some doctors refuse to treat transgender patients), community, dignity, courtesy, respect.

Once out of nature, it seems, we aren't allowed to take our place among natural things.

Many, though by no means all, of those most inclined to shun trans people for our failure to fit the "natural" binary of male and female belong to traditional religious communities, which read the first chapter of Genesis ("God made human beings in God's own image ... male and female God created them" [1:27]) as not only building the gender binary into the fabric of Creation but sanctifying it by linking it with "God's own image." The rabbis of the Talmudic era recognized that a literal reading of this verse—a reading that decreed that human beings could only be male or female—didn't fit the facts of human physiology, that some children are born with what we now call intersex conditions, with ambiguous genitals, genitals of both sexes, or genitals that made it hard to assign any sex at all. The rabbis approached this not as a problem of theology (are these babies made in the image of God?) but as a practical question: how did such people, whom they divided into two categories, *tumtum* and *androgynos*, fit into the rigorously gendered system of Jewish ritual law? In posing the question in these terms, the rabbis made it clear that they considered intersex Jews human and Jewish, bound by God's law, and part of Jewish community. Though they didn't say this, it must have been clear to them that though relatively rare, intersex conditions are natural, part of the range of human variation.

Like intersex people, trans people don't fit the binary template for humanity religious gender traditionalists see as decreed in Genesis I, but unlike intersex people, our difference isn't visible at birth or inscribed in sex-defining genitalia. Not only doesn't our difference seem natural, it doesn't seem real, in the sense that there is nothing but our feelings and actions to attest to it. But traditionally religious people build their lives around intense personal relationships with someone who is even worse at fitting into human categories or definitions of nature than we are: God.

Like many transgender children I've heard of, I had a close relationship with God, and even as a child, I knew that closeness was connected to my transgender identity. Because I lived in a body that didn't feel like mine, as a boy I was only pretending to be, I didn't feel that I existed—and that sense of non-existence enabled me to experience God as a palpable presence. I felt God with me, in me, I felt personally created by God (though I felt God had made a botch of it), I talked to God all the time, and had no doubt that God was listening.

My family was Jewish, but not religious, so I didn't have any theology or religious authority to tell me that I wrong, and despite the verse in Deuteronomy proclaiming God's abhorrence of those who crossdress, what I read in the Torah, the Hebrew Bible, seemed to confirm rather than challenge my intimate connection with God: we were both beings without bodily form or place in the natural order who were desperate to be loved by people who had both.[4]

It's hard for trans children to hold onto our relationships with God. As we grow up, most of us are taught that God isn't listening to or suffering with us. God, we learn, can only be found through religions, traditions and theologies that until recently were more or less universally agreed that God despises us.

Trans inclusion in religious communities lags far behind the still-contested inclusion of gay and lesbian people. But trans children today are growing up in a world in which there are more and more synagogues, churches, mosques and temples that will tolerate, accept and even welcome them. Every year, fewer trans people feel forced to choose between being true to their gender identities and true to their religions. Inclusion of transgender people, however, will require not only tolerance and accommodation from religious traditions; it will require profound theological and spiritual growth.

The work of disentangling religious conceptions of God from what was long seen as the "natural" domination of women by men has taken generations, and is still far from complete. But even religious communities that have renounced patriarchal gender hierarchy still struggle to conceive of God or humanity or the divine image Genesis tells us we share in terms that transcend, or expand, or blur, or destabilize, or otherwise escape the gender binary.

The gender binary is an idol planted in the Garden of Eden: we don't know what "in the image of God" means, but we know what "male and female" mean, and their loose connection in Genesis I prompts many religious traditionalists to see the gender binary as a concrete, natural link between God and humanity. To truly include transgender people within Abrahamic religious traditions, we have to shatter the idol of the gender binary and face the truth that trans people embody: the gender binary represents neither the nature of nature, the nature of humanity, nor the nature of God.

However radical this may seem in terms of religious belief, practice and community, this truth is as down-to-earth as my mudhole, where, without fuss or fanfare, binary human categories collide, collapse, and coalesce into more capacious, messier forms; where bullfrogs thrum amphibious hymns under gliding great blue herons; where someone who lives as a woman after a lifetime as a male whispers "Thank you, thank you, thank you" to a God who knows all about human gender and couldn't care less.

What We Talk About When We Talk About "Gender Dysphoria": An Address to Psychotherapists (2015)[5]

DURING ARGUMENTS she hoped would save our marriage by dissuading me from gender transition, my then-wife crystallized the diagnostic challenges presented by claims of transgender identity: "If you tell me you've always felt like a chicken," she asked, "should I start treating you like a chicken?" To her, when I declared that I had always felt female, as I had told her from time to time since we were sophomores in college, I was demonstrating not that I had a female gender identity but that I—a bearded, kippah-wearing middle-aged father of three who had been monogamously married for over two decades—was delusional. From my wife's perspective, my therapist's diagnosis of "gender dysphoria" seemed no different from a diagnosis of "chicken identity disorder." Clients who insist they can only live authentic lives by living as chickens, even though they will probably lose their jobs and be shunned by family, friends, and strangers if they live as chickens, are clearly suffering from some kind of psychological disorder. A therapist who affirms such clients' claims, who encourages them to dress like chickens, to observe and imitate the behavior of chickens, to alter their bodies to resemble those of chickens and begin to come out to others as chickens, shouldn't be a therapist, or, I suspect, a chicken farmer.

That's how my wife felt about my therapist: that by accepting my claims of female gender identity and supporting my transition from living as a man to living as a woman, she was exacerbating the very disorder with which she had diagnosed me, and encouraging me to destroy my life and the lives of who loved me. To her, it was clear that my therapist's job was to help me understand the root causes of my gender dysphoria, and either guide me to a healthy embrace of male identity or to help me accept that however I felt, I was and would always be a man. She saw a number of possible causes for what, to her, was my rejection of my male identity. My father had been always been emotionally withdrawn, and abruptly stopped talking to me when I was 21. If my father was my model of masculinity, of course I wouldn't want to believe I was a man. Or perhaps I was tired of the responsibilities and pressures that accompanied masculinity—supporting my family, dealing with yard-work and automobile malfunctions, pretending to be rational. My wife pointed out that I didn't need gender transition to work through these problems. Besides, if I thought being a woman was easier or better than being a man, then I obviously knew nothing about being a woman. By her lights, my desire to live as a woman proved I was really a man.

My ex-wife isn't a therapist, but her skepticism about transgender identity can also be found among therapists. Though I've been blessed with excellent therapists in the past decade, I encountered kinder, gentler variations of my ex's theories in earlier journeys through the therapeutic world. Even therapists who listened empathetically to my inarticulate, shame-hobbled efforts to explain what I meant by "feeling like a woman" weren't eager to explore those feelings. Consciously or unconsciously, they steered me toward more familiar ground. My father, as you can imagine, was a therapeutic goldmine, as was my intensely co-dependent marriage, and we could always while away our fifty-minute hours by talking about my chronic, intermittently suicidal, depression. Indeed, my earlier therapists seemed happy to talk about anything other than my gender, and didn't seem to notice that no matter how much I learned about my father, my marriage and my misery, I remained as depressed and intermittently suicidal as when our therapeutic relationships began.

Of course, those therapists had little in the way of resources to draw on. In the 1970's and 1980's, there was no internet, and few clinical source books like Arlene Ishtar Lev's invaluable *Transgender Emergence* (2004). But even when I went to a gender identity clinic (I was living in San Francisco), the therapist I encountered wasn't comfortable exploring gender identity issues. The moment I introduced myself as a transsexual—the first word I learned to describe my relation to gender and identity as a child, and for decades the only word I had—I was offered hormone replacement therapy and other practical support for making the transition from living as a man to living as a woman. My therapist was baffled when I said that I had come there not for hormones but to explore my gender identity, to better understand my lifelong sense of being female, its meaning, its consequences, and the possibilities it represented. If I was really transsexual, my therapist indicated, I should transition immediately; if I wasn't ready to do so, maybe I wasn't really transsexual.

It is always complicated to respond to gender identity issues. Gender is built into our language, our mores, our intimate relationships, our very modes of understanding ourselves, which means that all gender identities, including those that fit normative definitions of male and female, are bound up with socialization, childhood experience, fantasy, fear, shame, and often trauma.

Non-trans people grow up without having to worry about whether their internal sense of being male or female is shared by those around them. For them, the gender binary that identifies everyone as either male or female represents a powerful, though sometimes oppressive, system for understanding and expressing themselves and building relationships.

But binary gender has no place for transgender people. We grow up in a world that offers us no way of understanding our gender identities, no way of expressing them that will be intelligible to others. There is one exception: the widely familiar idea that transgender people are women or men "trapped" in the bodies of the opposite sex. This concept of identity was developed for transsexuals, people like me who identify with a binary gender that is the opposite of the one we were assigned on the basis of the sex of our bodies. Transsexuals represent only one of the many forms of gender identity gathered under the umbrella term "transgender." But even for transsexuals, the "I am an X trapped in a Y body" meme is an inadequate and confusing model of identity, as one well-meaning questioner demonstrated when, after after a talk I gave about my gender identity struggles, he asked, "Did you know you were a woman trapped in a man's body even when you were a child?" Of course not, I told him: when I was a child, I didn't have a man's body, and had no idea what it meant to be a woman.

But since this meme is the only model our culture offers for transgender identity, I, like many transsexuals, spent most of my life trying to use it to understand my gender identity. I was delighted by the idea that my sense of female gender identity meant that there was an authentic, fully developed girl or woman hidden within my male body, waiting for me to drop my vigilantly maintained male persona and reveal her. Unfortunately, though, I could never locate this girl or woman who was supposed to be hidden inside me. Since I didn't conclusively fit the "X in a Y body" model, I obsessively questioned my gender identity, asking myself if I really felt "like a girl," if I still felt "like a girl," whether I had perhaps felt something that proved I wasn't "like a girl" after all.

That anxiety—the fear that my true female self was always on the verge of vanishing—was exacerbated by my obsessive monitoring of my behavior to ensure that I wouldn't do anything that might suggest that I wasn't really the boy everyone thought I was. For as long as I can remember, I lived in fear that my female gender identity might be discovered, and that I would be shunned as a result, exiled from family, friendships, every corner of the neatly gendered world. But the more successful I was at passing as a boy, the more anxious I was that I might not "really" be a girl. The terms of the "I am an X trapped in a Y body" model decreed that my gender identity should consist only of a fully formed, unambiguously female self that existed independently of not only of my body but of any of the complexities of human development or relationship. There was no way I could squeeze my fragmented, constantly self-questioning consciousness, my robustly maintained male persona, and my robustly repressed female gender identity into this model. Did that mean I wasn't transsexual after all? That my sense of female gender was a delusion, or a lie? How could I tell?

From childhood through adulthood, I tormented myself with these questions, interminably searching my feelings, desires, fantasies and actions for a fully formed female self that somehow had come into being without ever being expressed in my actions or relationships. Such a self, of course, is impossible. Becoming a woman requires more than a female gender identification; it requires living that gender identity. I could never fulfill the requirements of the "I am an X in a Y body" model because I wasn't a boy or a girl, or a man or a woman; I was an anxiously self-monitoring, chronically depressed, intermittently suicidal person with a male body, a male persona, and a female gender identity I was too ashamed and afraid to express. There was, and is, no word for such a complexly gendered self, but there is a term for the suffering that results from having a relation to gender that is inexplicable to others: gender dysphoria.

There are now many more recognized forms of transgender and nonbinary identity than when I first sought therapy, and many more books and educational resources on the subject. But it is still hard for therapists to respond to clients' claims of transgender identity without implicitly or explicitly questioning our sense of who we are. Insurance companies, endocrinologists, surgeons and agencies issuing government IDs all require transgender people to present letters from therapists declaring that our claims to transgender identity are neither fraudulent, tentative, nor delusional—and to confirm that we have, and are being treated for, gender dysphoria. Therapists who take these letters seriously are required to engage in diagnostic processes that demand, if not skepticism toward transgender clients' claims to know who we are, at least suspension of belief until our soundness of mind and consistency of sense of identity has been established. But since transgender people live in a world that constantly and sometimes violently questions our identities, diagnostic skepticism can be alienating, wounding, and, to severely depressed or suicidal clients, may seem to confirm our worst fears about our prospects of being known and accepted as who we are.[6]

Moreover, while some clients experience transgender identity—that is, a sense of their own gender that doesn't fit the binary categories of male and female—as a "disorder," many do not, and transgender critics have long argued against the "pathologization" implied by the diagnosis of gender dysphoria. These critics see therapists as "gate-keepers," whose ability to help clients is limited to authorizing medical services and insurance coverage, and whose judgments are an affront to clients' dignity.

If therapists are merely gate-keepers for transgender clients, and "gender dysphoria" is merely a set of magic words required by doctors and insurance companies, therapy sessions should be few, brief and *pro forma*. If "gender dysphoria" refers to a psychological condition that can benefit from therapeutic intervention, therapists should engage in diagnosis and offer therapy as well as statements of authorization. But if claims of transgender identity indicate psychological disorder, why would therapists support medical treatment to modify clients' bodies to match "disordered" gender identities? And if trans identity does not constitute a disorder—if having a gender identification that is not simply male or female is not itself a problem—what is "gender dysphoria" a symptom of?

It is important to note that no matter how greatly I suffered from gender dysphoria, my female gender identification wasn't a disorder, a symptom, or an illness. It didn't need to be cured or solved; despite my misery, I never thought I would be better off without it, because that gender identification was always at the core of who I knew myself to be. The therapist who helped me through gender transition knew that her diagnosis of "gender dysphoria" referred not to my female gender identity, but to the psychological, social and developmental consequences of growing up with an identity I could not understand or express in the terms my culture offered. A diagnosis of gender dysphoria, then, is a diagnosis not just of an individual, but of a culture: the client diagnosed with gender dysphoria is manifesting the culture's failure to support the articulation, understanding, expression, development and integration of transgender selves.

Because I had no model of identity that encompassed and made sense of all aspects of myself, I constantly had to choose between identifying with my male body and persona, or with my invisible, inexplicable, carefully hidden female gender identification. That was a terrible choice to have to make, but it wasn't hard. My body was a thing that wasn't me. It was a thing that hurt and negated me, a thing I hurt and dissociated from to show how little it meant to me; my male persona was a leaden masquerade. But because I dissociated from my body and the life I lived, no matter how I fiercely I clung to my female gender identification, I rarely felt alive. I thought of myself as a ghost without a body, or a body without a soul. Around the age of six, I decided that the only way to live an authentic life would be to kill myself. If I couldn't be truly alive, at least I could be truly dead. Indeed, a better, braver, more honest person would have killed themselves already, I told myself for most of my first 45 years, as I waited to die, longed to die, planned to die, and failed to die.

As several therapists have pointed out, my suicidal fantasies represented a failure of the imagination, my inability to imagine how to live. Like other aspects of gender dysphoria, this symptom—my inability to imagine a whole, authentic life—was an individual manifestation of a cultural problem: my culture offered no sense of how to live a whole, authentic life as something other than male or female.

My gender therapist asked me in our first session whether anyone had ever taught me to be true to myself. No. No one had taught me to be true to myself, because no one could recognize or conceive the self to which I needed to be true. And though I wouldn't learn words like "transphobia" until middle age, even as a young child I knew I was living in a culture in which being true to myself would have terrible consequences. Whenever a teacher addressed a class as "boys and girls," whenever a sitcom got laughs premised on the utter incompatibility of men and women, whenever the image of man in a dress was presented as humiliating and ridiculous, my culture taught me that someone like me, someone with a male body and female gender identification, didn't, couldn't and shouldn't exist. No one taught me to be true to myself because my self was a contradiction in terms, an unimaginable short-circuiting of the distinction between male and female on which personal relationships, social order, and the very notion of being human depended.

No one could imagine the person I was, but, supported by the gender-binary-fostered assumption that anyone with a male body is necessarily a man, my wife, family, friends and colleagues readily imagined that the male persona I cowered behind was actually a person, that my detachment represented presence, that my smiling misery represented happiness.

Though my male persona was what we might call a collaborative fantasy, it was a robust and useful fantasy. I built friendships and a career upon it, and, with my wife, a marriage and a family. Those investments created intense pressure to maintain that persona, not just for practical but for moral reasons. A good father, a good husband, a good colleague, doesn't change genders, because changing genders unsettles, confuses and can feel like betrayal to those who are invested in our lives. My wife, to whom I came out as trans in college, didn't mince words when, in my mid-forties, I told her I was finding it hard to keep living as a man. I had lived as a male for my entire life, she said. Since I was clearly able to live as a man, no matter how depressed, dissociated, or suicidal I was, I owed it to everyone to continue to do so. To her, and to many people who have expressed similar views, I had a moral obligation *not* to be true to myself, because others' lives depended on my acting like a man.

I found it hard to argue with her, because I had told myself the same things for most of my life. Like many transgender people, I had internalized this inverted morality when I was a child: as long as I can remember, I believed that those I loved needed and depended on me to conceal and repress my female gender identity, needed me not to tell the truth, so that they could continue to believe I really was a boy or man.

The beliefs that I had no right to authenticity, that the truth about my self was not only shameful but harmful to those I loved, that to live as myself would be unconscionably selfish and violate values of family, community, and faith I held sacred, were major symptoms of my gender dysphoria. Like other symptoms, this inverted morality was an individual consequence of a collective failure to understand transgender identities as valid, authentic, subject to the usual standards of integrity and honesty. Even well-meaning, compassionate therapists may embrace this inverted morality, as a trans friend of mine found when, after years of suicidal depression, her first therapist told her in their first session that no matter what pain her inauthentic life as a man cost her, she owed it to her children to maintain it.

How could a therapist give such fabulously bad advice to a client who, in their first session, said she was on the verge of ending her life? More importantly, how could I and innumerable trans people give ourselves such advice, and waste decades erasing and sometimes killing ourselves in the name of goodness and love?

The answer, I believe, is that binary gender is so central to how we understand and relate to one another that for some people, transgender identities unsettle what are otherwise clear moral and social norms of relationship. Those who love trans people may nonetheless insist that we doom ourselves to anguished, inauthentic lives. Those who know us best may feel, when we come out as trans, that they don't know us at all. Religious leaders who have never met us may feel that our existence represents an attack on their beliefs; strangers we pass on the street may experience our appearance as an assault to their ways of life—and may respond by assaulting us. People who are otherwise the epitome of tact may, when first meeting transgender people, ask about our genitalia and what sort of surgeries we've had. In short, when faced with trans identities, non-trans people may manifest symptoms of what we might call "social gender dysphoria": disoriented, often aggressive responses to their sudden awareness of the inadequacy of binary gender categories, the lack of conventions, norms, and syntax they need to relate to people who are other than simply male or female, the sickening inability to make sense of the person standing before them as human.

Of course, the world has changed since my mid-twentieth century childhood. Most Americans, even in conservative communities, accept a much wider range of gender expression as "normal" than in the mid-1960s, though the range of acceptable gender expression for boys and men is much narrower than that for girls and women. (Few articles of traditionally male clothing cause a stir when women wear them, but most articles of traditionally female clothing tend to cause at least a mild case of social gender dysphoria when worn by boys or men.)

Transgender people have become much more visible in the last decade, and there are more and more places in which we are legally protected from discrimination. But the vast majority of Americans, even the most politically progressive, still have little understanding of gender identities that don't fit the binary categories of male and female. In much of the country, including, until a few years ago, my home state of Massachusetts, it is still legal to discriminate against transgender people; even where there are legal protections, visibly transgender people suffer abuse and harassment, unemployment, poverty and homelessness, and, all too often, assault and murder.

As a white, tenured professor commuting from my home in a progressive New England college town to a job in New York City, I had it easy when I came out as transgender. I only lost my marriage, my home, my best friend, custody of my children, my middle-class standard of living, and the support of my university, which couldn't fire me but forbade me to set foot on campus for a year. And despite how much the world has changed since I grew up, if I were growing up today, I would still grow up knowing that being true to myself could cost me much of what makes life worth living—and possibly life itself.

The high costs and ongoing risks of being openly trans contribute to what might otherwise seem a puzzling problem: even after we begin living as who we are, many transgender people, myself included, remain at risk of suicide. Even when we stop hating ourselves, others may continue to hate us; even when we accept ourselves, others may continue to reject us. When we finally show up as who we are, those who loved us may turn away or attack us. Though we may heal our individual gender dysphorias, we cannot heal the social gender dysphoria, the lack of understanding of transgender identities, that gave rise to our symptoms.

But there may be other reasons for our continued suicidality as well. Gender is so fundamental to identity and relationship that, contrary to the "I am X in a Y body" meme, it is difficult to develop whole, mature selves while repressing or hiding our gender identities. Aspects of ourselves that we don't express or manifest in relationships tend to be underdeveloped, tentative, vulnerable, sometimes child-like.

When I began living as myself—living as a woman—it felt like a miracle: I couldn't believe I could wake up every day as myself, dress as myself, be seen and known as myself, feel and taste and smell and hear and laugh and even suffer as myself. After a lifetime of feeling like a persona, a ghost, I was embodied and alive.

After eight-and-a-half years, being alive still feels like a miracle. But living as myself wasn't the end of my struggles to develop a whole, mature self: in many ways, it was the beginning of what I now recognize as a lifelong process of learning to recognize desires, make choices, and take responsibility for their consequences, and, above all, to show up, to be present in relationships, to acknowledge and embrace my place in the world.

At first, that process was overwhelming. After 45 years of dissociation from my body and my life, I had developed very little capacity to hold my feelings, and I had never allowed myself to feel very much. Once I was living as myself, I didn't want to dissociate from a body and life that suddenly felt like mine—and found myself drowning in feelings I didn't know how to handle. In response, I fell back on my old coping mechanisms, dissociation and suicidality. I was ecstatic that I had finally come to life, and bewildered that I was spending so much of that life as I had before: numbly imagining killing myself. I wasn't suffering from gender dysphoria anymore—my body and life finally reflected my female gender identification—but the damage of years of living as someone I wasn't would take years to heal. To do that healing, I first had to learn to commit myself to life.

In the years that I have been living as myself, I have done a lot of growing, not just in my gender expression, but in my relationships, my sense of myself as a human being, and my ability to hold, appreciate and learn from feelings that once overwhelmed me. Unlike many transgender people, I have had the stability, safety and support I needed to do that growing. Thanks to tenure, I had a secure income, and could afford a small but decent place to live. Because most people read me as a female, I have experienced relatively little of the harassment and none of the violence to which many transgender people are exposed. Because I am white, educated and middle class, the negative reactions I have experienced to my trans identity aren't compounded by racism and class discrimination. Because I live in a progressive New England college town, I am only a little afraid when I have dealings with officials or professionals to whom I have to reveal my transgender identity. Because I am remarried to someone who loves me as I am, no matter how rejected by the world I might feel, I know there is someone in whose arms I will be safe. Without such blessings and privileges, the challenges of growing into a new self are much harder, the prospects of a creating a stable, fulfilling life more distant, the dangers of depression, despair and suicidality much greater.

You can't give your clients a world that welcomes them, any more than their understanding and acceptance of themselves can magically foster understanding and acceptance in others. But when you help them recover from gender dysphoria, your clients—through their relationships, their dignity, their courage in being true to themselves even when others don't understand the selves they are being true to—spur our culture to grow beyond the limitations of binary gender. One friendship, one family, one workplace at a time, they inspire new, more capacious, generous ways of understanding ourselves and one another. By insisting on being who they are, they challenge all of us to recognize and remember that humanity, theirs and ours, is infinitely more important than gender.

"We Pass for What We Are":
Otherness and Humanness
(2021)[7]

Not long after I began living as myself—living the lifelong female gender identification I hid until my mid-forties—I gave the first of what are now more than a hundred invited talks about gender transition and trans identity to groups who had little familiarity with life beyond binary gender. After four-and-a-half decades in the closet, I was still uncomfortable talking publicly about trans identity, and presenting myself not as a male persona but as who I really was.

Like many an uncomfortable speaker, I tried to put myself at ease by making a joke of my discomfort. "Hi, I'm Joy Ladin, and I'll be your transsexual this evening," I said, playing on the introductory formula ubiquitous among wait-staff in the San Francisco restaurant scene I sampled in the 1980s.

I thought of this "joke" as an attempt to set my audience and myself at ease by naming my gender difference and defining the relationship which, for an evening, gave me, as a trans person, a place among them. But now I see it as the opposite: as a way of presenting myself that showed I knew I was being seen as other, that I was in fact offering myself to serve in that capacity, as representative of a certain form of otherness.

At the time, I didn't distinguish between being trans and being other. As a result, I didn't see the difference that I called "being trans-sexual" as one among many gendered ways of being human. I saw it as a sign that I was *other*, different in ways that made me incomprehensible, unlovable, with no place in my family or community.

That terror had led me to hide my female gender identification for most of my life, which is why I reached for humor when I started speaking publicly about trans identity. If the audience would laugh with me, perhaps my difference and my otherness need not be so terrifying after all.

But in a way it has taken me years to understand, that joke was more than a fumbling attempt to defuse my childhood fears. It was also an effort to formulate a new, less isolating way of understanding the relationship between difference and otherness, to suggest that my otherness was not essential, an unavoidable consequence of being different in the way I was different: like being a waiter in a California cuisine restaurant, it was temporary, situational, a role I was performing for an evening for the benefit of those who wanted me to serve insight into trans identity and experience. Moreover, by saying I was *their* transsexual, I was asserting, in a way that felt quite daring at the time, that like a waiter's difference from the diners they serve, my difference gave me a place among them. For one evening, at least, being transsexual didn't make me other; it made me theirs.

In short, through this absurd equation (being trans is not at all like being a waiter), I was trying to reframe my otherness, to understand it not as an unbridgeable gulf that separated me from humanity, but as a basis for relationship.

Needless to say, one throwaway line wasn't enough for anyone, including me, to transcend the complex social and psychological dynamics through which difference becomes entangled with otherness. It didn't even get a laugh. I soon stopped repeating that "joke," but I kept trying to understand and articulate the experience of being seen as, and seeing oneself as, other.

For much of my life, I thought of otherness as a singular, undifferentiated condition. But I now recognize that I have experienced at least three distinct forms of otherness, which I call structural otherness, internalized otherness, and inherent otherness. Each is produced by different social dynamics, and produces different psychological and emotional effects; but all represent efforts to understand myself in ways that enable me to relate and connect to those to whom my difference marks me as other.

As a long-time therapy client, I have found that even the most experienced, insightful therapists have little language to distinguish, describe, or discuss experiences of otherness. That has made it hard for them to recognize, and help me recognize, the profound effects of growing up believing that I was other, much less to help me to understand the social processes that produced that belief and the psychological mechanisms I developed to cope with it. They couldn't prepare me for the shock of being seen as other after gender transition, teach me to navigate the practical, social, and emotional obstacle course that comes with that territory, or guide me in how to develop a healthy sense of self and belonging in a world in which, for the most part, people who are different as I am different are still treated as other. Nor could they help me identify and understand my internal experiences of otherness, or enable me to distinguish between my reactions to being seen as other (that is, reactions to structural otherness), the belief in my own otherness I internalized while growing up in binary gender world that had no category other than other for people like me, and the inherent sense of otherness, the inescapable sense of difference, that is the birthright of every human being.

Though it has taken me years to understand this, I now see that when I introduced myself as "your transsexual this evening," I was acting out and trying to overcome each of those kinds of otherness: my awareness that binary gender norms would prompt the audience to see me as other; my excruciating internalized belief that my gender difference made me truly, essentially other; and the sense of otherness that haunts every human being, reminding us that any place we have in the world is temporary, that there is nowhere we are fully seen or understood, that we never completely belong.

Though the experiences of otherness I describe below grew out of my inability to fit or make sense in terms of binary gender categories, the subject of this essay is not trans identity or being transgender. It is an effort to use my own experiences of gender difference to help enrich the language of otherness, regardless of the differences that give rise to it: to help us distinguish the varieties, wellsprings and effects of otherness, and to understand it simultaneously as a social circumstance many of us need to cope with, a psychic wound many of us need to heal, and what Emily Dickinson called "the Maker of the Soul," a formative, foundational sense of difference which, even as it makes us feel absolutely alone, gives us something in common with everyone around us.

1. STRUCTURAL OTHERNESS

When I began speaking publicly about transgender identity and experience, it was hard for me to distinguish between being different and being other, because I grew up believing that my gender difference, my combination of male body and female gender identification, meant that I was essentially other, someone—something—that had no place in family, community, or humanity.

But as a growing body of scholarship emphasizes, human differences, no matter how striking they seem, do not have to be interpreted as marking an individual as other. For example, even in the rigidly gendered world I grew up in, what we now call "the gender binary"—practices based on the assumption that every human being is either male or female—interpreted differences that distinguished between men and women not as signs of otherness, but as the opposite: signs that individuals belonged to and were filling the places assigned to them by the binary gender world. It was only certain kinds of difference, such as homosexuality, or cross-dressing, that the gender binary system prompted us to interpret as signs of otherness.

Otherness is not built into or produced by being different from those around us. Otherness is a way certain differences are interpreted by the systems (or, as some academics call them, "discourses") of gender, race, economic class, and so on that we rely on to identify ourselves and those around us. As Jean-Francois Staszak explains, this kind of otherness

> is the result of a discursive process by which a dominant in-group ("Us," the Self) constructs one or many dominated out-groups ("Them," Other) by stigmatizing a difference—real or imagined—presented as a negation of identity and thus a motive for potential discrimination. To state it naively, difference belongs to the realm of fact and otherness belongs to the realm of discourse.[8]

In other words, no one, no matter how they different they seem, is "really" other; otherness is in the eyes, and the identity-defining discourses, of those who see them as other. To use Staszak's terms, when I introduced myself as "your transsexual," I was not only announcing the fact of my difference. I was telling my audience that I saw them as members of a "dominant in-group" and that I knew the "discursive process" of in-group identification with regard to binary gender would lead them to see me as other.

I call this effect, which is the focus of many diversity, equity and inclusion efforts as well as many academic studies, "structural otherness." Even when it occurs in one-to-one relationships, as when a doctor or therapist sees a client who is different from themselves in some way as other, structural otherness is not personal. It is a consequence of our participation in groups, communities, institutions, or cultures that teach us to interpret certain characteristics as signs of who is "us," and who is other. That is why, as Staszak explains, structural otherness "is due less to the difference of the Other than to the point of view and the discourse of the person who perceives the Other as such." The otherness we see in someone who is different is not a perception of them at all. It is an effect of the discourses on which we rely to identify one another, or rather, of the blind spot that is a built-in feature of every identity-defining discourse, all of which limit our recognition of who is "us" to those we see as sharing certain characteristics with us.

Since human beings are social animals, all of us are hard-wired to internalize identity-defining discourses. Both as we are growing up and when, as adults, we join new groups or institutions, we learn to identify ourselves in terms of the discourses that, in a given context, define who belongs and who does not. The more foundational these discourses are to our culture, the longer they persist over time, and the more widely they are reflected in and reproduced by our institutions, the harder it is to shake the sense that differences such as skin color, or religion, or ethnicity make people really, essentially "other"—and to recognize their otherness as our interpretation rather than a facet of their being. And the more accustomed we are to believing that this or that difference "really" means that someone is other, the more pervasively that belief is reflected and reproduced by our families, communities, and culture, the harder it is to recognize and empathize with the humanity of those whose differences we interpret as otherness.

I now see that my little self-introductory joke reflected a naive belief—a wish—that simply being self-aware of the discursive process that turned my gender difference into a sign of otherness would enable me and my audience to transcend it, to stand together outside the discourse of binary gender and regard it from the standpoint of a common humanity beyond it. As a fellow poet, Chen Chen, pointed out to me some years ago, this sort of universalist fantasy is common among white people like me, because, as Staszak would say, the discourse of race teaches us to interpret whiteness not as a kind of difference but as the default condition of humanity. Chen was right: even though I grew up feeling absolutely other due to my gender difference, I also grew up equating whiteness with humanity, and so, paradoxically, believed that in some ways, my perspective was, or should be, universal.

Chen reminded me that no one, including people like me who are often seen as other, is free of or from the assumptions and distortions built into identity-defining discourses. Cultures and societies depend on these discourses to define roles, identities, and communities; they are embodied in and reproduced by institutions, policies, and etiquette; individuals internalize them as part of acculturation, and, even when we recognize or suffer from their shortcomings, we habitually rely on them to understand who we are in relation to others, and who others are in relation to us. That's why, even when I'm giving a talk about the shortcomings of discourses of binary gender that do not include people like me, I still unconsciously use that discourse as I scan the audience, automatically sorting the people I see, as I have my whole life, into men and women. Neither studying binary gender discourse nor being stigmatized and marginalized because of it have enabled me to erase it from my mind, or to stop relying on it to identify and relate to the people around me.

But the fact that we cannot be free of identify-defining discourses does not mean that we must be prisoners of them. Even if we cannot dismantle the structures that promote and sustain them, we can learn to become conscious of how these discourses prompt us to interpret differences and remember, when we see someone as other, that what we are seeing is a projection of ideas that sustain our own sense of who we are, and that those ideas are preventing us from recognizing the person standing in front of us—their reality, their individuality, their humanity.

2. INTERNALIZED OTHERNESS

Identifying structural otherness has helped me recognize my responses to being seen as other—feeling simultaneously over-exposed and invisible, disregarded and judged, completely vulnerable and threatening to the social order, profoundly isolated and lumped into the general category of "people like *that*." It helps me notice the rage, frustration, loneliness and helplessness I feel in those situations, and the shame and guilt threaded through them, the sense that I am to blame for being something that those around me cannot help but see as other. And being aware that these feelings are not signs of psychological disorder within me but a reaction to social processes around me, processes I cannot control or avoid, enables me to focus on navigating social situations in ways that protect me from, or at least minimize, the stress of being seen as other.

But understanding structural otherness doesn't help me understand why, decades before I started living my transgender identity, I saw myself as other. From early childhood, I believed both that I was really, essentially female, and, just as passionately, that I was really, essentially other—perhaps a stranded alien, or a ghost haunting a body and life that weren't mine, or a monster, or a divine mistake, but certainly not a part of the human world where everyone else, it seemed to me, was simply, purely, male or female.

For most of my life, I lacked the conceptual tools I needed to understand this sense of internalized otherness. None of the few autobiographical accounts of transsexual lives I found as I wrestled with gender dysphoria and tried to decide what to do about it spoke about the feeling of otherness which has always been entangled with my what I now call my trans identity. Written to explain and defend gender transition to a skeptical, hostile binary world, the accounts I read emphasized that trans people's gender identities were like those of non-trans people, just as consistent, just as essential to who they knew themselves to be.

When I started privately coming out as trans—including to therapists—that's the way I described myself too. The still-popular "I am an X in a Y body" formula—the idea that there is, or should be, no difference other than physical between the gender identities of trans and non-trans people—was the only recognized model of trans selfhood, the only language that would persuade even those who were most supportive to accept my female gender identification as authentic, as a "true self" that I should be allowed to live.[9]

I presented myself in these terms to get access to treatment, to try to explain the mysterious experience of gender dysphoria to family and friends, and to try to justify the process of gender transition that I knew would disrupt my spouse's and children's lives and destroy the family we had created. But I always knew that by leaving out my sense of internalized otherness, I was editing out an important aspect of my trans identity and experience—and now, I would say, editing out important an aspect of my humanity.

It wasn't until I read W.E.B. Du Bois's pioneering work of phenomenology and sociology, *The Souls of Black Folks*, that I found, in his concept of "double-consciousness," a way to understand my internalized otherness. Du Bois, of course, developed this concept to describe Black American identity, not transgender identity; the identity-defining—or identity-negating—binary whose effects he articulates divides human beings into black and white rather than male and female. His most widely-known description of double consciousness appears in a phenomenological account of how an archetypal Black American "him" makes sense of himself in an American world structured in terms of a discourse that interprets light skin as a sign of citizenship and humanity and dark skin as a sign of otherness:

> ... [T]his American world ... yields him no self-consciousness, but only lets him see himself through the revelation of the other [white] world. It is a peculiar sensation, this double-consciousness, this sense of always looking at one's self through the eyes of others, of measuring one's soul by the tape of a world that looks on in amused contempt and pity. One feels his two-ness,—an American, a Negro; two

souls, two thoughts, two unreconciled strivings; two war-
ring ideals in one dark body, whose dogged strength alone
keeps it from being torn asunder.[10]

As Du Bois makes clear, double-consciousness—"always looking at
one's self through the eyes of others"—is a response to the structural
otherness promoted by institutionalized racism, a cognitive discipline
adopted in order to survive and navigate the white American world.
The discipline of constantly seeing oneself simultaneously from the
inside and the outside, of "always" remembering how white people see
Black people, not only offers practical advantages in terms of anticipat-
ing and trying to avoid the vileness and violence of white supremacy; it
also offers psychological, social, and political insights, which Du Bois
elsewhere calls "second sight," that are beyond the ken of those who
have always been seen as white.

Du Bois describes double consciousness as a way not only to survive and "see through" the white supremacist structures of American
society but also to identify as a Black American in a world that equates
"American" with "white." That is one reason double consciousness
comes at such a high psychological cost. It not only entails always
remembering how white people see Black people; it entails internalizing this toxic racial discourse, "measuring one's soul" by its contemptuous standards, and thus internalizing the sense that to be oneself is
also, always, to be other. This sense of otherness is not just in the eyes
and minds, institutions and interpretive discourses of those who interact with us; it becomes part and parcel of the way we think of and
"measure" ourselves.

As a result, this internalized sense of otherness becomes hard to
separate from the sense of being ourselves, and the sense of being ourselves becomes hard to separate from the sense of being other.

My white, late-twentieth-century life as a closeted trans person
had little in common with the lives and souls of Black folk Du Bois
was describing. But his concept of double consciousness gave me a
way to recognize my own lifelong sense of "two-ness," my simulta-
neous sense of myself as female (and thus someone who belonged
in the world of binary gender) and as other, and to see it as an

effect of the double consciousness I practiced in order to hide my trans identity.

I remember schooling myself in this form of double consciousness—training myself to always look at myself through the eyes of binary gender—as early as first grade. During the day, I would monitor and police my gender expression to ensure that I would "pass" as the boy everyone thought I was, and at night I would criticize myself for the ways in which, despite my efforts, I struggled to fit in. To remain attached to my family, friends, and community, I knew they had to see me as someone I wasn't, which meant that I had to avoid behavior that might give away my female gender identification. It's hard for anyone to live in the closet, but it is especially hard for a child. In order to ensure my words, actions, and body language fit what was expected of a boy, I constantly reminded myself of how incomprehensibly, unlovably other I would seem if anyone ever glimpsed my female gender identification, ever glimpsed, that is, me as I knew myself.

I survived and remained attached to the world of binary gender by internalizing its transphobia, a discipline analogous to the way Du Bois describes Black Americans as surviving and remaining attached to a white supremacist America by internalizing and measuring themselves by its racist standards. And so, as Du Bois would say, I "ever felt my two-ness," the struggle between the part of myself that cherished my female gender identification as who I really was even though I knew that those around me would see it as deviance or delusion, and the part that subjected me to a constant stream of transphobia to ensure I never said a word or moved a muscle to express it.

By my mid-forties, the psychological toll of this regimen of double consciousness became so great that I could no longer continue living as a man. When I started living as my true self—living my female gender identification, while acknowledging my life as a male—I finally experienced the structural otherness I had avoided by hiding behind my male persona. Despite the stares, stigma, and loss of housing and job security that often accompany structural otherness, being seen as other brought a kind of relief. For the first time, otherness was no longer something I was doing to myself, an exercise in psychic self-mutilation I performed to fit into the world of binary gender. It was now a sign that I, me as I knew myself, was part of that world, and had a place, however uncomfortable and dangerous, in it. And unlike internalized otherness, which made me feel singular and isolated, being seen as other meant that my gender difference now connected me to the community of trans and non-binary people marginalized by the discourse of binary gender.

The structural otherness I experienced when I began living as myself enabled me to relax into a form of double consciousness more like that which Du Bois describes, a way of seeing myself that enabled me to claim a place, however problematic, in the world of binary gender, and to anticipate and navigate the reactions of those who saw me as other. When I introduced myself by saying, "I'm Joy Ladin, and I will be your transsexual this evening," I was expressing this double consciousness, and inviting my audience to share it with me: to join me in simultaneously seeing me as an individual, "Joy Ladin," and as a transsexual other. Laughing at that joke, I hoped, would magically move all of us to a perspective that was both inside and outside binary gender discourse, a perspective from which we could laugh at its limitations and recognize the humanity we shared behind and beyond it.

Du Bois, and anyone else who has lived with structural otherness, would know better than to indulge in such wishful thinking. No matter how precisely, passionately, or playfully we invite those who see us as other to share the perspective double consciousness gives us, no matter how many jokes we tell or speeches we give or books we write about it, words alone can't dissolve structural otherness or the discourses that produce it. If they did, *The Souls of Black Folks* would have ended white supremacy long ago.

This is not just a limitation of language; it is a limitation of double consciousness. As Du Bois knew, for all the insight and perspective we may glean from it, as long as we engage in double consciousness, we reproduce the discourse whose effects we are trying to survive, locating ourselves within it by identifying ourselves in its terms and living in ways shaped by the knowledge that we are seen as other.

Some people escape the trap of double consciousness by abandoning the effort to attach to and identify themselves as part of societies that define them as other: they form separatist movements, like the Back to Africa movement, or lesbian separatism, or the early versions of European Zionism, embracing identity-defining discourses that interpret their shared characteristics not as signs that they are other but as proof that they are Us. Others, like those who champion queer identities, escape double consciousness by inverting the values that dominant discourses assign to their differences, embracing otherness as a form of liberation, a way of rejecting the oppressive hierarchies those discourses sustain and embracing more capacious forms of humanity than those discourses offer even to those who live comfortably within them.

I've never wanted to separate myself from or live in opposition to the binary gender world; I have accepted the danger and discomfort of living as other within it as the price I pay for being a parent, a teacher, a public speaker and writer. But I've also never felt at home in this way of life, which requires constant awareness of the possibility of violence or rejection by anyone who is uncomfortable with transgender identities or bodies. I steel myself for possible harassment whenever I use a women's room, and enter and leave as quickly and invisibly as I can; I adjust my voice and body language that help me "pass" as a non-trans woman in casual interactions; when I see doctors or other strangers who need to know I am transgender, I prepare myself for unpredictable reactions, awkward questions, signs of discomfort, inappropriate assumptions, and the occasional outright hostility.

Like queer activists, I value my otherness as a source of insight and possibility, and, like separatists, I long to feel connected to people not despite but because of who I am. As a result, even after I learned to live with being seen as other, I kept looking for a way to make the universalizing wish I expressed in those early self-introductions come true, for a perspective from which otherness could be recognized not just as a product of oppression and double consciousness but as a sign of a shared humanity.

3. "WE PASS FOR WHAT WE ARE": INHERENT OTHERNESS

Unlike the Black American experience of double-consciousness Du Bois describes, the double consciousness that enabled me to live as a male wasn't a response to the way my difference was interpreted by those around me, or to living in a society founded on and paid for by oppressing people like me. No one could see that I was different, and even once I read of their existence, it was many years before I met other trans or non-binary people.

As a result, I didn't experience my otherness as an effect of social oppression that connected me to people like me. When, in order to survive and attach to the world around me, I internalized binary gender discourse, I internalized the sense that my otherness was absolute, that "other" was simply what I was, an inescapable consequence of a gender difference that set me apart from the rest of humanity.

Even after gender transition, after I had formed relationships in which I was seen and loved as the person I know myself to be, I found it hard to shake the sense of internalized otherness that had, for most of my life, simultaneously cut me off from and enabled me to attach to the world of binary gender. Binary gender is still the basis of most people's identities and relationships. Identifying others as either male or female still determines who most of us see as potential sexual or romantic partners, how we understand our children, divide family chores, choose our friends, evaluate clothing and careers, decide where to walk at night, how to interact when stuck in a crowded elevator. And the discourse of binary gender continued to live in me, as I relied on the habits of double consciousness that had enabled me to maintain my male persona in order to navigate the world that now saw me as other.

So it wasn't surprising that a sense of internalized otherness persisted long after I stopped hiding and started living as who I really am. But unlike the feeling of being absolutely other that I grew up with, the internalized otherness we experience when we rely on double consciousness also offers connection to people who are different in the same way we are. It fosters a sense of kinship with those who, like us, are subjected to segregation, discrimination or other effects of structural otherness.

As I made a life as an openly transgender person, I experienced that sense of kinship with other trans and non-binary people, and also formed intimate relationships with non-trans people who didn't see me or require me to see myself as other. But despite these experiences of belonging, and despite years of effective (and much-needed) therapy, I was still dogged by a deep feeling of otherness, a feeling that didn't seem directly connected to gender at all, but seemed to be part and parcel of who I was.

I call this feeling "inherent otherness." As I see it, inherent otherness can be experienced by anyone, regardless of social position. No matter how comfortably ensconced we are in institutions and social structures that tell us we belong, we still may feel that there is something different about us, something that sets us apart from even the most rewarding roles and identities, something that has no name and that others cannot understand that reminds us that we are never exactly who we seem to be to others, something that, to put an anachronistic spin on Ralph Waldo Emerson's declaration in his famous essay "Self-Reliance," makes us feel that "we pass for what we are."[11]

When I was living as a man, I *was* passing for what I wasn't. But even after gender transition, I noticed that despite my efforts to live honestly, openly, and authentically, I couldn't shake the sense that I was still passing for who I was. At first I attributed that feeling to the fact I was not used to living my female gender identification; later, to living in and having to navigate a world that sees trans people as other. But eventually, I realized that *I* was the source of this sense of otherness: I felt other because, no matter how openly I lived my female gender identification or how fully accepted it was, there would always be ways in which I was different from the way I seemed to those around me.[12]

This otherness was not a psychological wound or effect of oppression. In ways it has taken years to understand, it was part of me.

I got my first glimpses of inherent otherness at the beginning of gender transition, when I started coming out to non-trans women who had befriended me as a man. I believed that these friends, unlike me, were "real" women, women who identified completely with the gender they were assigned at birth and felt no dissonance with or difference from their identities as adult women—who never felt that they were passing as the women they seemed to be. I saw them as living examples of what I longed to be, and what, according to the old-fashioned formulation that describes people like me as "women trapped in men's bodies," gender transition would enable me to become: a woman who, inside and out, fit comfortably into the discourse of binary gender and so would no longer feel that I was other.

But to my dismay, each of these friends, even the most heteronormative, responded to me coming out as transgender by telling me that despite being born and raised and living their lives as female, they too had struggled to feel like the women they were supposed to be—the women who, according to binary gender definitions, they really, essentially, inarguably were. Though each told me a different story, they all described hiding or repressing aspects of themselves in order to fit what was expected of them as women, and feeling, as a result, that they were always in some ways passing as the women they were supposed to be.

They seemed relieved to make these confessions, and to expect me to be relieved to hear them. After all, they were telling me that I wasn't alone in struggling to pass as what others expected women to be. But I wasn't looking to them for companionship in otherness; I wanted them to be real women who could welcome me as and help me become the real woman I longed to be. I didn't want to hear that even those born on the right side of the binary might still feel that, when it came to gender, they, like me, could only pass as women by hiding some of who they knew themselves to be.

When I starting speaking publicly about being transgender, more heteronormative people told me what my friends had said: that even though they were not transgender, they related to my descriptions of trying to pass and feeling other so deeply that they felt that the language I was using for my life applied directly to theirs. Some of the feelings of otherness they described were connected to gender, but many were not. I heard from elderly people who felt they were other than the way elderly people are supposed to be; people who first felt other because, though born and raised Christian, from an early age, they felt they really were Jews; and a couple whose loss of an only child made them feel other than the parents they were supposed to be.

As I had been with my women friends, I was reluctant to take in what these people were telling me: that even though their lives and situations were nothing like mine, they saw the otherness I described as something we had in common, a kinship independent of particular differences or experiences of being seen as other. I now realize that I've never spoken to anyone, no matter how well they seem to fit or perform their assigned roles and identities, who has said that they have never experienced such feelings.

This kind of otherness puzzled me. It wasn't structural otherness or the internalized otherness produced by double consciousness, since the differences that made those who described feeling other to me were not visible, nor was it an effect of alienation from rigid social roles (being seen as elderly, for example, isn't a rigid social role). These people felt other because they knew that there were aspects of themselves that didn't fit the way they were seen or expected to be, and so, like the female friends I came out to, they identified with my experiences of hiding who I knew myself to be in order to pass for who, from the outside, I "really" was. Just as, physically and in terms of social identity, I really was a boy and then man, the friends I came out to were really women; the elderly people were really elderly; the bereaved parents were really parents. Their feelings of otherness and sense that they were passing reflected a profound mismatch between the social interpretation of who they were and their private awareness of the fullness and complexity of their being, a being which included aspects of themselves that did not fit and could not be comprehended by the identity-defining discourses and social roles that connected them to those around them.

That is why I call this "inherent otherness": not just because I and those who have described it to me experience it as an inherent consequence of being who we are, but because the sense of being other than we are supposed to be is inherent in the nature of what human beings rather misleadingly call our identities. On the one hand, we develop our identities by internalizing and relating to others in terms of the identity-defining discourses we share with our families, communities, and cultures; on the other hand, as self-aware individuals, we identify ourselves based on what we know of our own complex, constantly changing feelings, desires, experiences and psyches. There is always a mismatch between who we are to others (our social identities) and who we are to ourselves (our self-identifications). We always know ourselves to be at least somewhat different on the inside than we seem to those around us, and that sense of difference—the sense that we do not "really," fully, permanently, essentially fit the social roles and identities through which we are known by and connected to others—gives rise to the sense that we are in some way inherently other.

Of course, the degree of slippage between social identity and self-identification, and so the intensity of the sense of inherent otherness, varies greatly, not only from one person to another, but also over the course of individuals' lives. People like me who are transgender or nonbinary or otherwise identify ourselves in ways that have no place in the identity-defining discourses into which we are socialized tend to experience an extreme mismatch between our self-identifications and our social identities, and are prone to feel, as I do, a high degree of inherent otherness. But for many people, the identities and roles available to them and thus the ways they are known to others fit tolerably well; though there is always some slippage, some dissonance, some ways they know themselves that don't fit how they are known by those around them, it isn't a major source of discomfort. As a result, those slippages, and the troubling, isolating sense of inherent otherness that accompany them, can be repressed, forgotten, rationalized, or, as the female friends who told me they didn't feel like real women explained to me, simply lived with, accepted as part of the cost of social identities whose rewards in terms of relationships and sense of belonging are far greater than the discomfort of the sense of otherness they entail.

And as I learned from the bereaved couple whose loss made them feel inherently other than the parents they were supposed to be, because human beings and human lives are constantly changing, even those who at one time feel they fit their social identities well may at another time experience excruciating dissonance between who they seem and who they know themselves to be. Before their child's death, that couple felt that they really, essentially, *were* parents in the ways that those around them expected and understood them to be. The consonance between their sense of themselves and their roles and identities as parents was a source of joy and of connection, not only in relating to their child, but in relating as parents to other parents, to their families, to their communities. When their child died, their internal sense of themselves as parents who were defined by their love for their child continued, but because, without a living child, they no longer fit the social roles and identity of parents, they felt they were no longer "real" parents. This excruciating experience of feeling that they both were and were not parents did not make sense in terms of the identity-defining discourse of the family; there are no social identities or roles or even names for being a parent whose child is dead. And so for years they had felt like they were only passing for parents, that they were really, inherently something other than what parents are supposed to be.

If my hypothesis is right—if the nature of humanity and identity are such that all of us experience slippage between who we are and who we are supposed to be, so that we are all to some degree living with the sense that we are inherently other—then otherness is not just a consequence of being seen as different, or of double consciousness or other psychological mechanisms for surviving oppression and marginalization. Otherness is an inescapable, indeed, a foundational, aspect of being human.

That makes otherness sound like an existential wound, or at least one of civilization's and consciousness' persistent discontents, something we experience only when we are unable to avoid it by immersing ourselves in the sense of belonging, or at least connection, that we get from conforming to the roles and identities through which others know us. Conformity minimizes our awareness of internal slippage between who we are and who we seem to be, prompting us to tailor our behavior to fit the roles and identities others know us by, so that we consistently act as though we are who we are supposed to be. And when we embrace those roles and identities internally—when we define ourselves in terms of the feelings, experiences and parts of ourselves that fit them—it becomes easier to ignore, repress, deny, or rationalize those which remind us that in one way or another we are other than we are supposed to be. When identification and conformity are not available to us—when what we know about ourselves (like feeling we really are Jewish despite being born and raised Christian) or what we experience (like losing a child) prevent us from immersing ourselves in the roles and identities that connect us to other people—it becomes hard to avoid the sense that we are inherently other than, and only passing for, what, as far as those around us are concerned, we are.

But despite the anxiety and isolation that many of us, including me, associate with it, in "Self-Reliance," Emerson celebrates inherent otherness. To him, the shifting, contradictory psyches that we hide by conforming to social roles and identities are not only our true selves, but the source of the individual "genius" that leads us to new philosophical, artistic, and religious breakthroughs. They are the outward sign and inward channel through which our individual souls express "the divine spirit," the cosmic Oneness Emerson sees as embracing and radiating through each of us. Thus, Emerson argues, it is morally, spiritually, and existentially imperative that we embrace our inherent otherness, and, no matter the social cost, live the aspects of ourselves that prevent us from fitting our assigned roles and identities, because only when we do so can we really be, and not just pass for, who we are.

Many contemporary queer and trans theorists and activists champion similar ideas, linking what Emerson calls "nonconformism" with authenticity, wholeness, integrity, vitality, insight, creativity, and personal and social transformation. Though "Self-Reliance" does not discuss gender nonconformity, and though these writers, to my knowledge, don't discuss Emerson, this common ground is not surprising. After all, gender nonconformity by definition requires us to embrace aspects of ourselves that make it impossible to conform with the binary gender world or be consistent with the roles and identities we were assigned at birth. And while these contemporary "nonconformists" tend to focus on people who identify as queer, trans or nonbinary, some echo Emerson in encouraging everyone to recognize how they don't fit assigned gender roles and identities and what it costs to conform to them.

But Emerson insists that no one ever truly fits *any* of our roles and identities, that, as we would say today, all of us are essentially queer, and that no matter how well individuals fit assigned roles and identities, no matter how exalted we are by them or how richly they benefit us, the costs of conformity always far outweigh the rewards. In a critique that rings uncomfortably true to my memories of passing as a man, Emerson writes that conformity "scatters [our] force ... and blurs the impression of [our] character," leads us to become "timid and apologetic" (97), and "makes [us] not false in a few particulars, authors of a few lies, but false in all particulars [so that our] every truth is not quite true" (87–88, 97). And according to Emerson, these are not passing effects; they are cumulative and degrading: "[N]ature is not slow to equip us in the prison-uniform of the party to which we adhere. We come to wear one cut of face and figure, and acquire by degrees the gentlest asinine expression ... the forced smile which we put on in company where we do not feel at ease in answer to conversation which does not interest us" (89). "Whoso would be a man," he declares, "must be a nonconformist" (83).

Those were fighting words in early nineteenth-century America, a paradoxical challenge to "man up" by refusing to conform to the conventions of maleness and other identity-defining discourses that place his assumed readers at the apex of the social pyramid. In Emerson's culture, one had to be a white, educated man to be seen as fully human; Emerson argues that to achieve full humanity, we have to express the shifting impulses, desires, contrarian opinions, self-contradictions and other idiosyncratic aspects of ourselves that would dislodge us from our assigned roles and identities and reveal us as truly, inherently other.

Of course, compared to those of us who occupy more tenuous or marginal social positions, it is relatively easy for Emerson to make this argument. Emerson takes for granted the privileges his social roles and identities confer, without regard to the ways those privileges might limit his understanding of humanity and society, the injustices that make those privileges possible, or the suffering of those excluded from them. That is why, though Emerson acknowledges that "For nonconformity the world whips you with its displeasure," he never considers the possibility that for some people, the risk of such violence was and still is literal rather than figurative, that conformity may not be a choice that shows deficient character but, as for many LGBTQ people today, a necessary means of survival (88).

But though he doesn't imagine what conformity might mean to those who, unlike him, have been or might be seen as structurally other, Emerson is quite aware of how following his advice and deciding to be a "nonconformist" may disrupt personal relationships. He even offers readers a model script for coming out as nonconformist to friends and family members whose lives will be most unsettled by that transition, a script whose content will be familiar to many LGBTQ people and those we have come out to:

> Say to them, O father, O mother, O wife, O brother, O friend, I have lived with you after appearances hitherto. Henceforward I am the truth's.... I shall endeavor to nourish my parents, to support my family, to be the chaste husband of one wife,—but these relations I must fill after a new and unprecedented way. I appeal from your customs. I must be myself. I cannot break myself any longer... If you can love me for what I am, we shall be the happier. If you cannot, I will still seek to deserve that you should. I will not hide my tastes or aversions. I will so trust that what is deep is holy, that I will do strongly before the sun and moon whatever inly rejoices me, and the heart appoints.... It is alike your interest, and mine, and all men's however long we have dwelt in lies, to live in truth. Does this sound harsh to-day? You will soon love what is dictated by your nature as well as mine, and, if we follow the truth, it will bring us out safe at last. (102–103)

Emerson's coming-out speech combines two arguments that are still common today: the "born this way" argument that we must live aspects of ourselves that we have previously hidden beneath conformity because they reflect our essential "nature"; and the "integrity" argument that, in order "to live in truth," we are morally and existentially required to express "deep" aspects of ourselves (including "our tastes and aversions"), no matter how problematic others may find them. And, like many contemporary versions, this coming-out speech insists that the decision to stop conforming and start "living in truth" does not mean we are rejecting family members and friends who assumed that we really were who we have long appeared to be.

But Emerson is more than an early adopter of the now-familiar (though far from universally accepted) ideas that people who are different in ways that are stigmatized should live as we know ourselves to be, that relationships should be based on truth rather than conformity, and that people should be loved for who we really are. When he instructs would-be nonconformists to tell those who feel hurt or angered by them that "You will soon love what is dictated by your nature as well as mine"—that is, that the speaker's coming-out will "soon" inspire them to embrace the aspects of themselves they are hiding in order to fit in—he asserts that no one's "nature" is served by conforming to social roles and identities, that even those who are most passionately attached to conformity are "naturally" inherently other than what they seem to be.

I can attest that Emerson vastly over-estimates the power of his words and nonconformists' actions to persuade most people to abandon accustomed roles and identities and embrace their inherent otherness. Indeed, though decades of passing as a man taught me the costs of conformity, even after my gender transition, I worked hard to conceal my otherness and "pass"—this is the term I used—as a non-trans woman. Despite having taught "Self-Reliance" every few semesters for years, I strove for the conformity Emerson excoriates, hoping that "living after appearances" would "blur the impression of [my] character" sufficiently for me to be seen as a woman instead of as a gender-complicated other.

Neither Emerson nor queer and trans theory nor the examples of my non-trans friends who came out to me as feeling they were passing for the women they were supposed to be could convince me to relax, much less abandon, my commitment to conformity. What led me to "love"—or at least accept—the otherness "dictated by my nature" was the reluctant realization that to pass as a woman who completely fit binary gender conventions, I would have to conceal, deny and cut myself off from every aspect of my life that contradicted them: abandon the children to whom I was a father and the mother to whom I was a son, disown the writing and teaching careers I had built before transition, and deny all that I done and felt, learned and experienced, suffered and enjoyed, as a boy and a man. In the name of living as a whole person rather than as a male persona, I would have to chop myself into pieces and exclude those that didn't fit the generic category of "woman."

Therapists used to demand that transsexual clients make such sacrifices in order to prove that our gender identities were real and not just fetishes or delusions. Doing so was a prerequisite for receiving hormones and gender-confirming surgeries, and, they believed, or claimed to believe, for a socially and psychologically successful gender transition. Fortunately, this form of cruelty masquerading as psychotherapy was discredited before I began working with a gender therapist. But it still took me years of striving to conform before I realized, as Emerson insists each of us should, that I needed to stop trying to fit the standards by which the binary gender world defines who is and isn't a woman, and focus instead on living my whole, messy, inconsistent, nonconforming truth—the truth that means that however well I may pass as a woman, I am and will always be inherently other.

At first this realization felt like an admission that I had failed to overcome the otherness I had always felt cut me off from humanity. But though he was wrong about how easily people can be convinced to embrace nonconformity, Emerson is right that when we don't, human beings pass for what we are. To belong to families, clans, communities, organizations, institutions and cultures, we have to conform to the identity-defining discourses that assign us places within them, and repress, suppress, or deny any "tastes or aversions" or other aspects of ourselves that would keep us from being seen as one of Us. To enjoy the social, economic and psychological benefits of belonging, we always need, in some degree, to pass for the kinds of people those around us expect us to be—which means that Emerson is right in assuming that each of us, to one degree or another, experiences inherent otherness.

Contrary to my lifelong assumption, my sense of inherent otherness was not caused by my gender difference, but by what Emerson reminds us is the inevitable mismatch between the roles and identities that relate us to those around us and the messy, constantly changing flux of our individual psyches. We aren't inherently other because of any specific way in which we are different. The same characteristic that is interpreted as otherness in one context may be seen as essential for belonging to another, as I learned when, after transition, I moved between gender-binary-based institutions like my university where being openly trans marked me as other, and LGBTQ groups where trans identity made me one of Us. No matter what our characteristics or social context, there are always parts of us that do not fit the roles and identities we are assigned, and so, no matter how comfortable we feel or how successfully we conform, we are always inherently other.[13]

I suspect that this sense of inherent otherness—or rather, the desire to escape inherent otherness by projecting it out of the self—is one of the reasons why so many of us, including me, willingly participate in discourses and social structures that interpret certain differences as signs of otherness, and why so many of us, including me, are so susceptible to feeling othered—to internalizing the sense that we are other—when we are on the receiving end of structural otherness.

But inherent otherness is not only a source of vulnerability to damaging social pressures. It is also a site of resistance to them, a sense that reminds us that we are never limited to or defined by the roles and identities to which we are assigned; that no matter how insistently identity-defining discourses put us in our places, no matter how brutal or seamless the systems that enforce them or how powerful the incentives to conform, we can always be more, and other, because whether we like it or not, we *are* always more and other, than what those discourses say we are.

Whether we treat it as a source of strength or weakness, recognizing that there are aspects of ourselves that make us inherently other does not mean, as I feared, that we are too different to belong. It means we are awakening to what it means to be human.

That's what those non-trans friends and audience members were trying to tell me: that the sense of otherness that made me feel so alone is something we all have in common, the painful, glorious birthright, the "genius," as Emerson might say, of humanity.

II

TRANS AND OTHER WOMEN

Confessions of
a Born-Bad Mother
(2014)

HOW BAD a mother am I?

So bad my children call me "Daddy."

It's not my fault. I was born to be a bad mother. My bad-mother-hood is literally written in my genes, in the form of the Y chromosome that waves its helplessly male arms in every cell of my body, waiting futilely to be replaced by the second X chromosome that would transform me from a male-to-female transsexual into a real woman.

During the fifteen years that I lived as a married heterosexual father, the name "Daddy" was an honorific, a public sign of my love for my children and my children's love for me. But even then, I felt like a bad mother. No matter how many miles I walked with babies or toddlers strapped to my chest, cradled in my arms or swaying on my shoulders, no matter how many diapers I changed, meals I cooked, dishes I washed, no matter how many hours I waited to pee after a long drive in order to meet the endless stream of pent-up childhood demands for food, play, and attention, I could never move the needle on the meter of good motherhood, because I wasn't and never would be a mother.

It wasn't my fault that I wasn't a mother. I didn't ask to be born male, and I never wanted the uterus-less body I inexplicably found myself inhabiting. But as my wife's body, pregnancy books, and every mention of motherhood reminded me, my XY chromosomes rendered me incapable of either enduring the burdens or achieving the miracles of female reproduction. Menstruation, pregnancy, miscarriage, childbirth, nursing, the suffering they entail, and the courage they demand, were constitutionally beyond me.

But it wasn't just biology that marked me as a bad mother. My maternal inadequacy was a social given whenever I mingled with mothers, which I often did when I took my small children to day care, preschool, or playgrounds. When mothers were talking mom-to-mom, I couldn't join in without disrupting the conversation, like a shaggy dog bounding up to be petted. Even in the egalitarian college-town venues in which I did pickups, drop offs, playdates, and parties, my biology was my social destiny: I might be recognized by mothers (the ultimate judges) as "a great dad," but the top of the fatherhood scale fell well short of the lowest rung of true motherhood.

Being a dad among moms has its perks, of course. I was praised for even the smallest parental involvement: Look, he changes diapers! Wipes drool! Soothes screaming infants! No matter how equally my wife and I shared family chores, my wife's mothering was constantly being measured against her peers', but no one judged me on the quality of our kids' diets or the creativity of their birthday parties. Since the social as well as biological burden of good motherhood always fell squarely on her, despite her feminist critiques and commitments, my wife accepted feeding the children, clothing them, educating them and so on as her personal responsibilities. And since she had been raised female and I had been raised male, we both agreed that she was infinitely more capable than I was of handling aesthetics, details, and planning. Though I did much of the shopping, cooking, and cleaning up, she decided what we would eat and how it would be prepared. Even when I dressed the kids, she laid out the clothes—and seemed authentically horrified on the rare occasions when I dared to put together an outfit. Though I did most of the grocery shopping (with children in tow), she assembled the lists I relied on—which meant that she planned all the meals and kept track of everyone's needs and supplies. As the social standard of good mothering demanded, she took on the mental work of parenting, from noticing who needed a new toothbrush to evaluating school choices. Following the social definition of good fathering, I "helped," spending hours discussing household concerns as our children multiplied. But we both believed that no matter how mentally capable I might be in my professional life, my fatherly brain was simply not sharp enough, my grasp of my children's needs simply not clear enough, for me to be entrusted with planning, scheduling, remembering, noticing.

Don't get me wrong. I loved the aspects of parenting that fell to me. To this day, years after living apart from my children, my body aches to feel a small body squirming against it. Had I actually been a man, I probably would have been gratified when mothers, including mine, said I was "so good with the kids"—but this phrase, bestowed as a high compliment on fathers, would be an insult to any mother. A father who's good with kids is considered a great father; a mother who's good with kids is considered . . . a mother. And though I never envied my wife the interminable work of thinking about household concerns, the oft-repeated self-fulfilling prophecy of my male incapacity for it sealed my sense of maternal inadequacy.

But the maternal inadequacy represented by being a "good dad" was nothing compared to the disaster that followed my transition to living as a woman. There's no scale of parenting values in which gender transition is a plus—and most non-transexual onlookers consider it a sign of abject, irremediable failure. No matter what I did for or with my children, I was no longer in the running to be considered a good parent of either gender once I started presenting myself as a woman.

My children told me, frequently, that I could never be their mother because they already had one; my eight-year-old daughter shared her opinion that my transition made me a bad role model for my then-fourteen-year-old son. There was even a legal presumption that gender transition made me a bad parent: When my wife filed for divorce, I was subjected to a court investigation to determine if my transition made me a danger to my children. The lengthy psychologist's report officially decided that though transition made me too self-absorbed to be a good parent, I wasn't dangerous because I would do what my therapist told me to do. Though it was my wife who filed for divorce and argued that I should have limited contact with my children, the law treated me as a father abandoning his family, a twist on the usual paternal selfishness and incontinence, though in my case it was wearing women's clothing rather than having an affair or gambling that I was putting ahead of my children's needs. Other than a few friends, my therapist, and my attorney, no one seemed to believe that I had delayed transition until it was the only alternative to suicide, and that I had endured years of anguish and isolation because I couldn't bear to leave my children. Like most parents whose transition precipitates divorce, I lost physical custody and was entitled to see my children only three times a week.

Needless to say, at no point in this process was my wife's quality as a parent in question, both because she wasn't trans, and because, as many courts still believe, children are better off with their mother. In fact, my transition increased my wife's good-mother quotient. She was seen as a heroic single mother, bravely soldiering on after the devastating betrayal of their father, a man so feckless he literally wouldn't keep his pants on for the sake of his children. Even though she had initiated the divorce, everyone knew the breakup was my fault.

But I have never fought harder or suffered more for love of my children than after my new life as a woman won me the gold medal for maternal failure. Like many transsexuals, I felt as though I had been reborn: For the first time in almost fifty years, I walked the world as the person I knew myself to be. Like every newborn, I wanted my miraculous new self to be loved, held, cherished. But that, of course, wasn't how my children saw it. To them, my new self wasn't a miracle; it was a catastrophe that had destroyed their home, their lives, their world. Even today, when new relationships and lives have risen from the rubble, they wish that I—the real, female me—had never been born.

There's nothing unusual about my children's feelings. It's easy for a noncustodial parent in an acrimonious divorce to become demonized, a repository for the rage all children feel when adults who should be caring for them inexplicably disrupt their lives. When the reason for such a divorce is gender transition, it's hard for children to distinguish transition from divorce, their trans parent's emergence into the light of day from the shattering of their home. No matter what I did when I was with them, I had utterly failed them as a parent. No matter how they begged, I wouldn't go back to living as a man, or living with their real—they would say only—mother. No matter how they wept when I left, I still left. No matter how much they longed for me, I wasn't there to murmur to them when they had trouble falling asleep, comfort their nightmares, kiss them awake in the morning.

Everything I knew and loved about being their parent had been stripped away; all that was left was showing up. Whenever I had a chance to see them, I did, erasing my fledgling female self by assuming once more the clothes and voice of a man. No matter how broken my heart felt, I gazed with love into their stony faces, gave hugs and kisses that weren't returned, waited patiently for them to look at, talk to, and play with me. I sobbed every time I left them. I hated myself for not being with them, for failing to be able to be the man they mourned and missed, for surviving living apart from them.

I became an unnameable kind of parent, a parent defined wholly by negations: noncustodial, non-male, not a mother, no longer a father, not present enough, not invisible enough, not a danger but definitely not good in any way. No one knew what someone in my position should do or should be; all anyone could tell me, from friends to therapists and rabbis, was that no matter how angry my children were or how much I hurt, I had to be there for them, whenever and however I could. And so I was, day after day, year after year, while new forms of relationships and love grew around the wounds of transition and divorce that would always be there.

Even after five years of healing, I am still in some ways nameless. "Mama" is their mother, their very good mother, and I am—they aren't quite sure. Usually they call me "Daddy" and "he," but sometimes pronouns slip, and recently my older daughter told me that when I referred to myself as "father" in a card I wrote her, it felt wrong and strange. She didn't know what other word to use, because our words and relationships with parents are so deeply enmeshed with gender, there is no name for what I am to her.

My children—and they are not the only ones—need another word for parent, one that means that however we fail or succeed at our gendered roles of father or mother, we love them utterly, and forever.

"I am She as You are She as You are Me and We are All Together": The Politics of Identifying as a Woman

(Based on a lecture given at Mount Holyoke College, 2015)

IF YOU READ the comment threads responding to articles on trans issues published online, you will probably notice violent exchanges between anti-trans feminists and conservatives who feel their own identities violated when trans women identify ourselves as women, and trans women who feel erased when anyone denies that we are women. Beneath these ferocious battles over what "woman" means is the unspoken agreement that anyone who defines "woman" differently than the authors is committing violence against—if not threatening the existence of—them and everyone like them.[14]

In a world in which both trans and non-trans women face institutionalized discrimination, hostile legislation, and physical violence, why do strangers' definitions of "woman" feel so dangerous? Why would non-trans women feel their identities, supported by what is still a largely binary-gender world, threatened by the way trans women, a tiny downtrodden minority, identify ourselves? And why would trans women, accustomed to asserting who we are in a world that tolerates us at best and often acts as though we don't and shouldn't exist, feel threatened by a few more digital denials, however hurtful they may be?

To explore these questions, I want to examine one of my own experiences of the online battle over who is and isn't a woman. Trigger warning: I am about to take anti-trans comments seriously. Anyone who doesn't want to do that should stop reading now.

In March 2012, the *Huffington Post* published a chapter from my memoir of gender transition. The original title of the chapter was "Being a Man"; they changed it to "Transgender: Why I Chose to Become a Woman," and were rewarded with a torrent of online comments, many of which objected to the idea that anyone not born female could "choose to become a woman." One of the most detailed came from Rose Verbena, a self-identified lesbian, expressing views I've heard not only from anti-trans feminists but from conservative women who would be appalled to think they had anything in common with either lesbians or feminists. According to Rose Verbena,

> The man in this story—like every other "trans woman"—is a biological male.... That's what he is. Male. There's nothing he can do about that but accept it. If he wants to cross-dress or behave in non-masculine ways, who is stopping him? But he will never be a woman, because he's male.... Lesbians have had enough of MEN "mansplaining" to us what it means to be a woman. News flash, guys: you'll never know. Because you'll never, ever be one.

According to Rose Verbena and many who argue against the validity of trans women's identities, physical sex and gender identity are inextricably linked. If I am biologically male—and no matter how long I live as a woman, every cell of my body will always include a Y chromosome—then I can "never be a woman."

It's easy to point out that Rose Verbena is confusing two different things, and that gender (as any lesbian should know) is a cultural construct, while sex is a biological condition. But Rose Verbena speaks for many when she insists that the term "woman" refers to an essential fusion of biology, socialization, and personal history. When Rose Verbena says she is a woman, she is referring to an identity forged over a life lived as someone born, raised, and always seen as female.

Even if she were to admit that biology doesn't determine gender, Rose Verbena might argue that being a woman is inseparable from one's biology, because biology both gives women experiences physically male people like me cannot have (such as menstruation, pregnancy, and the risk of unwanted pregnancy) and assigns us from birth to socially constructed gender categories that crucially shape our lives. Moreover, while Rose Verbena has no choice but to be a woman, no matter what that identity brings her, she sees me as exercising the ultimate in male privilege by not only choosing to present myself as a woman but demanding that she and others who were born, raised and have always lived as girls and women change their definitions of woman to include me as one of them.

This isn't just a matter of gender theory or political ideology. If Rose Verbena has to accept me as a woman, then there won't be any public women's-only spaces in which she and others born female can be sure they won't encounter people they see as men. A sexual abuse survivor explained it to me bluntly: "I want to know," she said, "that when I go to a women's space, I won't see anyone who reminds me of my abusers." For women like her, the presence of people who are physically male represents not only the memory but the threat of violence—the very kind of threat they seek safety from in women's-only spaces. In this sense, and in many others, accepting someone like me as a woman redefines "woman" in ways that affects everyone who identifies as a woman.

But Rose Verbena's comment doesn't discuss the real-world consequences of how we define "woman." Her objections to the idea that "woman" includes people like me are deeper, more existential, than that. To her, my claim to be a woman undermines the meaning of a term that is foundational to her identity as a lesbian and a person.

It's easy to dismiss Rose Verbena and those who share her views. I can ignore them, as my therapist suggested, or ridicule them, as others on the comment thread did; I could censor them, demanding that they be expunged from comment threads on my essays and that those who made them be blocked; I could name and shame them as transphobes on social media, or even—as too many do—verbally abuse them in my own comments or threaten them with violence.

But to realize how easy it is dismiss Rose Verbena's views is to realize how little actual power voices like hers have over my life. Rose Verbena's comment didn't stop me from living as a woman, or keep others from accepting my gender identity; her words didn't enact legislation preventing me from using public restrooms, or inspire mobs to assault me.

Moreover, I don't want to dismiss Rose Verbena's comment, because, despite the profound differences in what we mean by "woman," Rose Verbena and I have lot in common. Like her, I see the category "woman" as central to my identity and my life, and like Rose Verbena, I become enraged when others define "woman" in ways that contradict what "woman" means to me. To both of us, assertions of female gender identity represent an extraordinarily powerful form of language—language that we use to define who we are, how we live, how we relate to others, and where we belong in the world.

When I say "I am a woman," neither Rose Verbena nor anyone else is compelled to recognize or treat me as a woman; by the same token, I am not transformed into a man when Rose Verbena calls me a man. Both Rose Verbena and I depend on the word "woman" to constitute our identities, but neither of us can compel others to accept what we mean by "woman."

It's hard to talk about the language of gender identity without triggering the kind of conflicts we see so often online. To examine how this kind of language works without tripping any cultural landmines, let me turn to a fictional declaration of gender identity: the first line of the Beatles' song, "I am the Walrus," which begins "I am he as you are he as you are me and we are all together." Since I hate saying "I am he" even for pedagogical purposes, I will take the liberty of rewriting the line as "I am she as you are she as you are me and we are all together."

This peculiar sentence exemplifies how the language of gender identity works. "I am she" is both a declaration of who I am in myself, and a declaration of who I am in relation to others. That combination constitutes my gender identity. But as "I am she as you are she as you are me" makes clear, when we constitute our gender identities, we are not only defining who we are, but defining those with whom we identify ourselves. When I declare "I am she," I am saying that "I am she" in the same way as "you" [others who identify as she] are "she," which means that, with respect gender identity, I am saying that anyone who identifies as "she" is "me," that with regard to gender identity, we are the same. That's what socially shared identity is: an assertion that despite how different individuals are, with regard to a certain characteristic, we are the same, or, as John Lennon put it, "all together," connected by the identity-constituting terms we share.

That isn't a problem as long as everyone agrees on what it means to be "she," but as feminists have discovered with respect not only to male-to-female transsexuals but women from different economic classes, races, ethnicities and cultures, even people who have two X chromosomes and no Y chromosomes may have very different definitions of what it means to be a woman. Those differences dog every effort to constitute women as a single, homogeneous political group.[15]

When I say "I am she"—when I constitute my identity by claiming an essential similarity to and kinship with others who say "I am she"—Rose Verbena finds my declaration both delusional and insulting, given our differences in biology, socialization, and personal history. But what really upsets her—what feels like a violent violation to her—is that when I say "I am she," she also hears me as saying "you are me," defining not only who I am but who she is, insisting that she and I are "all together" in womanhood. Unlike virulently anti-trans people, Rose Verbena says she doesn't care what my personal, idiosyncratic relation to gender might be ("If he wants to cross-dress or behave in non-masculine ways, who is stopping him?"). But Rose Verbena doesn't want my gender identity to define hers. That's why she experiences my saying "I am she" as "sexist" and "oppressive."

I am not trying to oppress Rose Verbena by presenting myself as a woman, and Rose Verbena, as she makes clear, isn't trying to oppress me. But the constitutive nature of declarations of gender identity means that, for better and for worse, all of us who say "I am she" are claiming to be "all together" with everyone else who constitutes their gender using the same terms. As a result, to many anti-trans women, when I identify as a woman, I am undermining, erasing, or forcibly redefining their identities as women.

Views like Rose Verbena's are often dismissed as "gender essentialism." But like Rose Verbena, when I say "I am she," I am expressing a gender identity that I too experience as an essential, unalterable given of my existence. For me, the fact that my female gender identification is at odds with my body and male socialization proves how essential it is to me: if I could have changed my gender identification to fit my body and social role, I would have, because it was so hard, so dangerous, and so seemingly crazy to insist, despite all the available evidence, that "I am she." So while I disagree that gender is essentially physical sex, like Rose Verbena, I embrace a form of essentialism, one that locates the essence of gender in my own sense of identity.

Of course, as Rose Verbena points out, there are many ways in which I differ from her and the vast majority of people who identify as women. Before I began living as a woman, my private sense of female gender identification was all that supported my lifelong sense that "I am she." Even as a child, I was acutely aware that I had no way to tell if this sense of being female was anything like that of people who were born and raised that way. I spent much of my life examining my feelings in a desperate attempt to determine whether and how I was like non-trans girls and women.

Once I began to live as a woman, my anxieties shifted from essence to performance: could I talk, move, think, love, write, dress, and otherwise live in ways that proved I was a "real" woman, that, now that I was living my female gender identification, I was she as other shes are she?

The answer, of course, was "no." Though my performance of femininity was soon sufficient for others to see me as a woman, after a year or two, I realized that nothing I did could prove that my sense of being female was the same as anyone else's. I also realized that no matter how deeply I feel that "I am she," I will never be "she" in the same way as those who were born, raised and have always lived as female.

But though Rose Verbena has more in common with the majority of those who say "I am she" than I do, those similarities are not as great nor as universal as she assumes. While many of those who Rose Verbena accepts as women have uteruses, breasts, menstrual cycles, bodies that produce much more estrogen than testosterone, etc., many, for one reason or another, do not. Moreover, the roles assigned to girls and women vary so greatly by class, ethnicity, community, religion, and so on that being born and raised female guarantees nothing in terms of what experiences or oppression any particular women may share.

And as I'm sure she knows, when Rose Verbena says "I am she," she means something different than the "I am she" of heteronormative women, a difference made clear later in the *Huff Post* comment thread when a self-identified conservative Christian woman said I wasn't a "real woman" because I would never know what it was to spend my life cooking and cleaning for an unappreciative man. For those whose definition of "woman" includes heterosexuality, Rose Verbena's identification as a lesbian means that she, like me, is not a "real woman."

And while online arguments focus on the differences between trans and non-trans women, the conflicts between Rose Verbena and me over whether people like me can say "I am she" grow out of something we have in common: our old-fashioned commitments to defining ourselves in terms of binary gender, to being, and being recognized, as women, despite what that means in a patriarchal, misogynist culture. While both of us want to change that culture, both of us rely on binary gender to understand and express who we are, and to identify our commitments, our comrades, our communities.

Some would argue that people like Rose Verbena and me would be much better off (and have much less to fight about) if we all stopped identifying ourselves in terms of binary gender. If we could "smash the gender binary," as some call for, or at least declare it obsolete, no one would have to fight over who is a man and who is a woman, worry about measuring up to gender expectations, or suffer misogynist oppression.

This is a utopian idea, by which I mean not that it is ideal, but that it is, for the foreseeable future, impossible. No one can simply erase categories of identity on which people have long relied to define themselves and others. Today, there are upwards of seven billion people on this planet who identify as male or female; even if we *could* smash the gender binary, we would be violating billions of people's right to define and express those identities. To me, that sounds more like totalitarian oppression than liberation.

But what if, instead of smashing binary gender, we focus on freeing individuals to define and express whatever identities they choose? Rose Verbena and I could define "woman" however we please, without forcing anyone else to accept our definitions. Everyone, trans and non-trans, binary and nonbinary, could embrace any gender identity they please.

This idea is not utopian. It has been put into practice by many groups and institutions that welcome those who identify as trans or nonbinary, most famously in the ritual of declaring pronoun preferences when introducing oneself. By declaring their preferred pronouns, each individual determines, names and expresses their gender identities however they choose at any given moment.

When we engage in this practice, we agree that rather than inferring individuals' gender identities from how they look or act, as binary gender accustoms us to doing, we will accept whatever genders individuals declare, whether they fit our ideas of gender or not. In theory, this means that everyone is free to identify and be accepted as the gender they choose, without implying, as Rose Verbena and I do when we say "I am she," anything about what gender means to anyone else. If Rose Verbena and I sat side by side and declared the same pronoun preferences, each of us, it would be understood, could mean something completely different by "she." There would be no shared system of gender to say that we—everyone who embraced she/her pronouns—are "all together."

But although treating gender as purely individual and self-determined defuses conflicts over what it means to be a woman, it does so by gutting the power of gender as a shared language, a language that enables individuals to define and express who we are in ways that relate us to others and which others understand. Some people, like those who happily identify as nonbinary, embrace the unintelligibility of identities that are purely self-determined, or at least accept it as a necessary price of the freedom to be exactly who they are. But there are many people—most of the human race, including progressives as well as conservatives—who, like Rose Verbena and me, want not only to be free to express our identities, but for others to understand, and for some to share, the identities we express, who want to say "I am" in ways that enable us to be "all together."

Thus far, there has been little recognition of this form of gender diversity—of the fact that not only do some individuals identify in ways other than male or female, but that individuals and groups may have fundamentally different ideas of gender, including binary gender. Reckoning with this kind of diversity requires more than respecting trans and nonbinary identities. It requires us to recognize and accommodate the many, sometimes conflicting ways individuals and communities live gender, including the anti-trans lesbian feminism of Rose Verbena, the religious and cultural gender conservatism of my Christian critic, the way people like me identify in binary terms even though we do not fit traditional binary categories, and the ways some people identify without regard to binary gender at all.

For examples of how this might work when it comes to the highly charged conflicts such as how to define "woman," we can look to women's colleges, institutions founded on traditional binary definitions of "woman" that have struggled with whether and how to include transgender and nonbinary students who don't fit those definitions. Different institutions have different policies, and those policies may change in response to the ongoing transformation of gender, but Mount Holyoke's admissions policy as presented on the college website's FAQ circa 2015 offers a usefully detailed example of how an institution based on a binary gender term can include those who embrace conflicting definitions of that term:[16]

Mount Holyoke College's policy on the admission of transgender students states that it welcomes applications for its undergraduate program from any qualified student who is female or identifies as a woman. Can you clarify "who is female or identifies as a woman"?

The following academically qualified students can apply for admission consideration:
Biologically born female; identifies as a woman
Biologically born female; identifies as a man
Biologically born female; identifies as other/they/ze
Biologically born female; does not identify as either woman or man
Biologically born male; identifies as woman
Biologically born male; identifies as other/they/ze and when "other/they" identity includes woman
Biologically born with both male and female anatomy (Intersex); identifies as a woman

The following academically qualified students cannot apply for admission consideration:
Biologically born male; identifies as man

This policy acknowledges that there are many different ways to define "woman," but instead of treating them as mutually exclusive, as fights between trans and anti-trans women do, it accepts all of them as qualifying applicants for admission to a women's college. This list combines binary-based definitions (albeit presented in a way which, unlike traditional binary definitions, distinguishes between physical sex and individual gender identification) with definitions that rest on individualist understandings of gender (such as " identifies as other/they/ze and when 'other/they' identity includes woman") that defy conventional binary assumptions and cannot be expressed in binary terms. Rather than trying to determine which way of doing gender defines "woman" correctly, it signals Mount Holyoke's broad acceptance of not only diversity in individual applicants' gender identities, but of ways of understanding and expressing gender. And instead of focusing on the differences and conflicts between those ways, it identifies a unifying common ground, something all these ways of doing gender agree on: to be accepted to a women's college, one cannot both be physically male and identify as a man.

This policy did not make Mount Holyoke a gender paradise. Some students admitted under this policy want to be identified as women, some want not to be, and some do not want their declarations of womanhood to imply that they are "all together" with those who have conflicting definitions of woman. Some feel empowered by pronoun-identification rituals, some annoyed, some feel put on the spot and some feel erased. And sometimes, as we saw in the widely-publicized conflict over whether "The Vagina Monologues" should be performed at the school—some students saw it as is transphobic, because it equates womanhood with biology, while others hailed it as a feminist landmark, because it breaks taboos against non-trans women speaking frankly about their bodies and their lives—these conflicts escalate into fights to impose a single definition of woman.

But even at their worst, such conflicts do not mean that those who embrace different ways of doing gender cannot live together; they show that despite their differences, students continue to see themselves as a part of a larger community, one they fear may yet define gender in ways that exclude them.

Such anxieties may never go away, but we can allay them by managing conflicts among different ways of living gender the same way that we have learned to manage other conflicts between different ways of life: by ensuring that all parties feel their concerns have been listened to, understood, and respected; by focusing specifically on the areas of friction and what is at stake in them, rather than focusing on larger, irresolvable disagreements over gender and identity; by identifying common ground and values; and by negotiating compromises that may leave everyone dissatisfied but that address all their concerns. In addition to defusing the crises of the moment, properly managing conflicts can foster mutual understanding and respect, and reduce fears that accepting others' ways of life will erase or devalue our own.

In other words, we are not starting from scratch when it comes to accommodating diversity in ways of living gender. The history of religious conflicts out of which, in part, the United States grew, gives us centuries of experience of living with those who disagree with us about the basic terms of human existence. That history shows that such disagreements can't be resolved through proselytizing, learned debates, scientific research, forced conversion, or wars of extermination. Rather than fighting to the death over which religion is right and which is wrong, most of us have learned to live in a world that includes people who understand what it means to be human in very different ways than we do.

Gender is not religion, but the same reasoning holds when it comes to conflicts over gender. There will never be a single universal way of doing gender. Even binary gender is practiced in radically different ways by different communities and traditions, as we see when comparing comments by Rose Verbena and the Christian woman, whose understandings of gender have little in common beyond seeing it as determined by physical sex and being outraged that people like me call ourselves women. Not only *can* "woman" mean different things to different people, it always does, has and will as long as "woman" is part of the vocabulary of gender.

To embrace gender diversity in this sense, we have to stop trying to resolve conflicts between different ways of doing gender, stop fighting over who is and isn't this or that, what pronouns are and aren't valid, who should and shouldn't be recognized and represented, and instead work on managing these conflicts. Rather than treating them as existential battles, we should treat them the way we do other conflicts we want to resolve: by identifying common ground, working to minimize and find compromises in areas of friction, and assuring all sides that their views are recognized and will be accommodated as much as possible, including (following the religious accommodation model) allowing for spaces, gatherings, and private institutions devoted to particular ways of doing gender, rather than requiring all spaces and gatherings to adhere to a single way. This requires all of us to listen to those who do gender differently than we do even when their ways feel profoundly wrong or hurtful to us, to try to understand their anxieties and concerns, and show that we are committed to extending to them the freedom we ourselves want to do gender in the way that makes sense to us.

That can be hard to do when we frame these conflicts in terms of civil rights such as equal access and protection, freedom of expression, freedom of religion, and so on. Of course, we have to be vigilant in safeguarding these rights. But no matter how apt the civil rights framework may be when we look at these conflicts from a legal or political perspective, framing conflicts over gender this way makes it harder to understand and address the differences, anxieties, and needs that give rise to them, because the language of civil rights implies that those who disagree with us are uncivilly wrong. The idea that only one way of doing gender (our way) is right, just, true, moral, common sense and so on turns conflicts between ways of doing gender into battles to the death, magnifying anxiety, vitriol, and misunderstandings, and hardening everyone's positions.

The more entrenched this dysfunctional dynamic becomes, the harder it is for those with different ways of doing gender to recognize the common ground that, as I hope I have shown with regard to Rose Verbena and me, is always there. Rose Verbena and I will never agree on what it means to say "I am she," but we both value female gender identity, the relationships that identity helps us build, the sense of solidarity with others that it fosters. We have both suffered for saying "I am she," and we have both persisted in the face of gender-based discrimination and violence in affirming our female gender identities. Even if Rose Verbena and I never feel that "we are all together," surely we can learn to live side by side; even even though I will never be she the way she is she, surely we can cooperate in efforts to fight violence against and improve the lives of people we identify as women.

It may take decades for our culture to learn to reckon with gender diversity, to develop laws, policies and social etiquette that assure everyone, regardless of gender identification or expression or way of doing gender, equal rights, protection, access, opportunities, and dignity. After all, we are still far from achieving these goals with respect to more familiar forms of difference, such as race and class, and, for that matter, binary gender.

But we don't need to wait for our culture to evolve in order to show respect, kindness, and compassion to those who see the world, including us, differently than we do. Humanity doesn't require us to settle conflicts over gender and identity; it requires us to recognize that, whatever our differences in how we understand ourselves and one another, "we are all together."

Diving into the Wreck:
Trans and Anti-Trans Feminism
(2017)

SHOULD PEOPLE LIKE ME, people who identify and live as women despite have been born, raised, and lived as male, be accepted as women?

That question has split feminists for over half a century.[17] On the one hand, as trans and trans supportive feminists argue, feminism is a movement that opposes the oppression built into traditional binary systems of gender—systems that divide humanity into males and females and give the former more power, more authority, more money, more attention, and more respect. By working to free women from the assumptions, inequities and limitations imposed on those on the female side of the binary, feminism has always embraced what Emi Koyama called the first principle of trans feminism, "that each individual has the right to define her or his own identity and to expect society to respect it."[18] From this perspective, trans women should as a matter of course be accepted (and our gender identities respected) by feminists working toward these goals.

But as anti-trans feminists (sometimes known as "gender critical feminists" or "trans-exclusionary radical feminists") have long pointed out, accepting trans women as women radically changes the meaning of "woman," the term that serves as the foundation of feminism. The biologically rooted, binary definition of "woman"—that a woman is someone who not only identifies as but was born, raised, and has always lived as female—has from the first served as the basis for feminists to argue that people born into vastly different cultures, gender systems, classes, ethnicities, races and religions can and should see themselves as sisters, united by shared experiences such as menstruation and pregnancy as well as male oppression. For these feminists, feminism's efforts to transform binary gender paradoxically depend on the binary-gender distinction between the men who are the beneficiaries of gender-based oppression and the women who suffer it. They see accepting trans women as women not as an outgrowth of feminism's liberatory purpose but as undermining the very terms, "men" and "women," "male" and "female," that enable feminists to identify gender-based oppression and unite to oppose it. That is why, in the increasingly heated culture wars and legislative battles over trans rights, we often find anti-trans feminists who oppose traditional patriarchal gender systems fighting on the same side as cultural and religious conservatives who support them. Though anti-trans feminists and conservatives disagree about many things, both see acceptance of trans women as women as threats to the binary gender distinctions on which their identities, institutions, and communities depend.

The belief that inclusion of trans women poses a threat to feminism and to the very existence of women as a distinct group can make anti-trans feminism hard to distinguish from transphobia. But as Elinor Burkett's widely-shared 2015 *New York Times* editorial, "What Makes a Woman?" showed, feminists who repudiate transphobia and oppose the oppression of transgender people may believe that there is an inherent opposition between trans and feminist ideas of gender, and that including trans women under feminism's intersectional umbrella weakens the feminist movement by blurring the unifying concept of "woman."[19]

For the trans and anti-trans feminists who engage in them, debates over the definition of "woman" are neither abstract nor academic. They are existential battles over who and what we—trans and non-trans women—individually and collectively are, where we belong, where we are safe, whom we are fighting with and what future we are fighting for. At stake are not only the answers to those important questions, but our right and our power to determine these crucial dimensions of our lives. That is why, all too often, the interaction of trans and anti-trans feminists is marked by hate speech, threats, exclusions and counter-exclusions, accusations and counter-accusations of violence and violation: because the conflict between trans and anti-trans feminism seems to be a zero-sum game, in which only one side—one definition of "woman"—can prevail.

The binary framing of this debate—the assumption that "woman" either does or doesn't, and that feminism either should or shouldn't, include people like me—dooms us to repeat the same worn and bitter talking points. Rather than further fuel this self- and mutually-defeating dynamic, in this essay, I want to "dive into the wreck," as Adrienne Rich's famous poem put it, to explore the submerged roots of the collision between trans feminism and anti-trans feminism from a perspective that enables those on both sides to

> ... see the wreck and not the story of the wreck
> the thing itself and not the myth
> the drowned face always staring
> toward the sun[20]

*

For trans and anti-trans feminists alike, "the story of the wreck" often begins with Janice Raymond's 1979 book-length polemic, *The Transsexual Empire: the Making of the She-Male*, which argued that people born male were not and could never become women, and that trans women (or, as Raymond calls us, "male-to-constructed females" or "she-males") who identify as feminists should be treated as patriarchal infiltrators threatening feminism from within.[21] Raymond's terms seem dated—even anti-trans feminists who, like Raymond, indulge in overtly transphobic hyperbole don't refer to "the transsexual empire" anymore. But as Burkett's "What Makes a Woman?" shows, even feminists who acknowledge that transgender people are oppressed and who at least nominally support transgender rights may share Raymond's view that trans women represent a threat to feminism:

> People who haven't lived their whole lives as women ... shouldn't get to define us. That's something men have been doing for much too long. And as much as I recognize and endorse the right of men to throw off the mantle of maleness, they cannot stake their claim to dignity as transgender people by trampling on mine as a woman.

For Burkett, as for Raymond, feminist recognition of trans women undermines the definition of "woman" on which feminist solidarity and critique of patriarchy is based by minimizing the role of female bodies and life experience in determining who is a woman, and empowering people born and raised male to claim, along with other privileges that go with being born and raised male, the privilege of redefining "woman" to fit our own needs.

For many trans women, these arguments are so hurtful that it is hard to consider them as arguments, even when they are presented in good faith rather than as asserted as self-evident truth or hurled as provocations. We have our own "story of the wreck," one that starts from experiencing maleness not as privilege but as a violation and erasure of who really we are. In this story, anti-trans feminists are oppressors rather than liberators, bullying supporters of a dehumanizing gender regime that holds that souls matter less than genitals and chromosomes, that no matter who we think are, we are in fact defined by the sex of our bodies. We are the heroes in this story, inheritors, defenders and extenders of feminism's centuries-long efforts to insist that biology is not destiny, that women should never be reduced to or defined by their bodies or others' ideas about what it means to be female. From this perspective, the inclusion of trans women doesn't threaten feminism; it saves feminism from collapsing into the kind of biological essentialism and determinism that many feminists have worked to refute, and from defending the very gender binary that perpetuates women's oppression.

*

Despite our very different stories about who is threatening and oppressing whom, trans and anti-trans feminists generally agree that we hold contradictory, mutually exclusive ideas about feminism, identity, womanhood, and gender. But as Talia Bettcher points out in "Intersexuality, Transgender, and Transsexuality," not only do these ideas have important similarities, but trans and anti-trans feminism, like the hands in M.C. Escher's famous etching, have always been intertwined with and shaped by one another.[22]

As Bettcher points out, we can see the kinship between trans and anti-trans feminisms in the ideas about gender and trans identity in Raymond's *Transsexual Empire* and the pioneering trans feminist work of Sandy Stone and Kate Bornstein:

There was agreement that the medical model of transsexuality serves to perpetuate sexist norms (Raymond 1979, 92; Stone 1991, 290), and that transsexuality is not a pathological condition but arises, rather, as a consequence of an oppressive gender system (Raymond 1979, 115; Bornstein 1994, 118). There was even agreement that bodily dysphoria, which motivates surgical intervention, would disappear in a culture that had no gender oppression (Raymond 1979, 119; Bornstein 1994, 70).[23]

According to Bettcher, these shared ideas, as well as the need to assert an alternative to anti-trans feminist definitions of female, and thus of gender, shaped what became the guiding assumption not only of trans feminism, but of most trans theory and activism; what Bettcher calls the "beyond-the-binary model," according to which gender should be individually determined rather than, as in binary gender systems, assigned on the basis of sex.[24]

The beyond-the-binary model's insistence that gender should be individually determined does not just contradict the anti-trans and traditional binary assumption that gender is determined by biology. By defining gender as something we determine for ourselves, the beyond-the-binary model also contradicts the idea (and, I would add, the fact) that for most people, gender is a socially shared system that enables us to identify ourselves in terms that relate us to others, fostering both personal relationships and collective endeavors such as feminism. According to Bettcher, the social understanding of gender is so foundational to feminist thought that trans feminists who insist on the beyond-the-binary model undermine their own efforts to convince other feminists that trans women's rights are integral to the liberation of all women.

The liberation of all women may seem like a utopian dream, but the contradictions between the beyond-the-binary and social models of gender are the source of many practical disagreements, including battles over women's spaces and events and who gets to share them, what gender language should be used by feminist organizations, and more technical questions, such as those discussed in a 2015 *New York*

Times editorial page debate about whether birth certificates should continue to record the sex of infants even though some of those infants will later identify in ways other than the sex to which they are assigned at birth. Transgender activist Tiq Milan, following the beyond-the-binary model, argued that birth certificates should no longer record sex:

> It's ringing true for many people that gender is self-determined and not something defined by a doctor or government agency. It makes the most sense to believe someone when they tell you their gender. I didn't choose to be labeled female at birth. That was a fixed idea based on the way a doctor viewed my body. I had no say in the matter. (Milan 2015)

Linda McClain, following the social model in the name of both feminism and demography, argued that we must continue to record sex on birth certificates in order to track and remedy sex-based discrimination:

> Whether it's male, female or other, there are legitimate reasons for using the category of "sex"; indeed, one powerful reason is to document, and fix, gaps in equality. Girls and women still experience discrimination and disadvantage on the basis of sex. (McClain 2015)

Both Milan and McClain agree that recording sex on birth certificates is highly consequential, but because their approaches to it reflect contradictory models of gender, they disagree about how, when, and why we should do so. If, following the beyond-the-binary model, we see gender as self-determined, then no one's gender should be assigned without their consent. But if we see gender as a social system whose inequities begin at birth, we need records that specify the gender by which infants were identified when they were born, regardless of how they may identify when they are older.

There is no obvious way to resolve this disagreement. Each answer is "right" in terms of the model of gender on which it is based, and each model reflects some but not all of the ways in which gender is lived. Though trans feminists have a tendency to equate opposition to treating gender as a matter of self-identification with transphobia and prejudice, as the debate over birth certificates shows, that opposition may also reflect the ongoing need to understand how gender is practiced in what is still a binary gender world.

*

Are Janice Raymond and her anti-trans sisters right? Is trans feminism an oxymoron, because trans liberation and feminist liberation are based on models of gender that inevitably undermine one another?

The answer, to my mind, is "no." In fact, I and many trans feminists follow Emi Koyama in pledging allegiance to *both* the social and beyond-the-binary models of gender, because each model underwrites key aspects of our identities. In order to identify as a trans woman—to base my identity on my sense of female gender identification rather than my male birth and socialization—I have to embrace the beyond-the-binary principle that gender is a matter of self-determination. But to express my female gender identification—to live and be seen and relate to others as a woman—I rely on the social model, using signs (such as female pronouns) that are socially defined to express my gender identity to others. Since my life as a trans woman depends on both models of gender, it is clear that even though those models are contradictory, they can also complement one another, fostering a richer understanding of gender and identity than either can promote on its own.

But to see them as complementary, we need to dive deeper into the wreck, past the mutually enraging stories of trans and anti-trans feminist battles over the definition of "woman," deep enough to recover "the drowned face always staring / toward the sun": the face of the feminism that is "drowned" by the conflict between its trans and anti-trans versions, and is "always" looking toward a light beyond it.

*

We glimpse that face in Rich's *Diving into the Wreck*, the 1973 collection which was not only a triumph and turning point for Rich as poet, but as Elizabeth Hirsh notes, marked a "constitutive moment in feminist self-expression."[25] Many of the poems in *Diving into the Wreck* directly or indirectly address gender, and most of those follow the social model, by which I mean they use terms such as "man" and "woman" in ways that assume these words have the stable, widely understood meanings binary gender assigns them. By following this model, poems like the widely anthologized "Trying to Talk with a Man" can concisely express Rich's views of men, women, and the struggles between them, because this model of gender assures us that members of either gender are similar to one another and different from the opposite gender in predictable, well-known ways.[26] So when we read Rich's title, "Trying to Talk to a Man," we know that we shouldn't read the speaker's communication difficulties as a personal problem but as a microcosm of communication between men and women in general. Since "man" and "woman" in this poem are socially rather than individually defined, the single man addressed in the poem represents all men, and the speaker's difficulties in trying to talk with him reflects difficulties all women face in talking with men.

But in the title poem, Rich leaves both the social model and binary gender behind. The speaker of "Diving into the Wreck" identifies as both "mermaid" and "merman," as "he" and "she," as what the speaker of another poem in this section of the collection, "The Stranger," would call an "androgyne":

> . . . I am here, the mermaid whose dark hair
> streams black, the merman in his armored body
> . . . .
> I am she: I am he
> whose drowned face sleeps with open eyes
> whose breasts still bear the stress
> whose silver, copper, vermeil cargo lies obscurely
>   inside barrels
> half-wedged and left to rot[27]

Compared with today's cornucopia of beyond-the-binary identities, Rich's "androgyne" seems dated, a simplistic combination of male and female signifiers used for theoretical and rhetorical purposes rather than as a representation of the actual lives or identities of trans (and, for that matter, intersex or nonbinary) people.[28] But for Rich, the male/female speaker represents an act of feminist imagination that enables the speaker (and, by extension, all of us) to rediscover and reclaim treasure that has been lost in the wreck of binary gender.

As Hirsch notes, Rich soon turned away from the androgyne and the possibilities of conceiving humanity beyond the binary that he/she represents: "Rich's next published volume, *The Dream of a Common Language*, turned back on such tropes, asserting, 'These are words I cannot choose again: *I humanism androgyny*' [1978, 66]."[29] Rich's change of attitude isn't surprising, given the fact that, as Jennifer Finney Boylan and other trans critics have pointed out, Rich, after *Diving into the Wreck*, not only "counseled Raymond during the writing of… *Transsexual Empire*" but is "credited by Raymond in the forward… as having provided 'constant encouragement.'"[30] By the time Rich was cheering on the composition of *The Transsexual Empire*, imagining a subject position that was neither simply male or female had come to seem incompatible with the anti-trans feminism she and Raymond shared—a form of feminism that sees beyond-the-binary ideas of gender as existential threats to the definition of "woman" on which feminism and feminist community depend.

But as Judith Butler's *Gender Trouble* points out, feminists don't need the presence or possibility of trans and nonbinary people to feel this kind of anxiety; the existential angst Raymond and other anti-trans feminists blame on trans women can be triggered by any feminist discussions of gender:

> Contemporary feminist debates over the meanings of gender lead time and again to a certain sense of trouble, as if the indeterminacy of gender might eventually culminate in the failure of feminism.[31]

I'm not sure what "debates over the meaning of gender" Butler has in mind, but feminism depends on the belief that binary gender can change and that feminists can change it, that feminism can not only redefine "man" and "woman" but demonstrate that whatever meaning we give them, the sex of our bodies does not determine who or what we, as individuals, are.

To be any sort of feminist is to insist that "female," "girl" and "woman" can mean something other than they have meant in the past, that girls and women can define themselves rather than being defined by the slow-changing binary gender system that underwrites and per- petuates others' ideas about what and who their bodies make them. Feminists may be troubled by the sense that gender is indeterminate, but it is the work of feminists—even anti-trans feminists—to promote that sense, to encourage everyone to see gender not as an inescapable prison in which we are all serving life sentences, but as a range of pos- sibilities, known and unknown, through which individuals discover and determine who we are.

When we recognize that feminist thought and efforts both depend upon and destabilize binary gender, we glimpse the kind of feminism that is too often lost in conflicts between trans and anti-trans femi- nists, a feminism that sees the social and beyond-the-binary models of gender not as threats to one another, but essential complements. The social model gives feminists widely shared binary gender terms with which to foster solidarity and activism—sisterhood—among those who live on the female side of the binary, and to critique gender as most people continue to live it. The beyond-the-binary model enables feminists to imagine and work toward ways of doing gender and ways of being human that are unthinkable in binary systems, ways in which individuals are not defined by physical sex.

Because feminism requires both social and beyond-the-binary thinking about gender, when we dive beneath the either/or, zero-sum rhetoric, we find a deep kinship between trans and anti-trans femi- nists. Both believe that we can and must remake traditional binary definitions of what it means to be a woman; both critique and resist patriarchal oppression and gender-based injustice and violence; and both see identifying as women as central to authenticity and libera- tion—to being, as trans people are wont to say, who we truly are.

Trans and anti-trans feminism are different sides of a capacious feminism that comprehends both. Even when the conflicts between them drown it out, that feminism never stops calling us to dive into the wreck and recover what feminists on each side lose without it. In Rich's "The Stranger," we hear this feminism loud and clear, a "living mind" indicting our "dead language" of either-or identities, reminding us of the inexhaustible possibilities that survive despite and within us, and of "the newborn child" of the future we can only make together:

> if they ask me my identity
> what can I say but
> I am the androgyne
> I am the living mind you fail to describe
> in your dead language
> the lost noun, the verb surviving
> only in the infinitive
> the letters of my name are written under the lids
> of the newborn child[32]

III

TRANS AND OTHER ACTS OF SELF CREATION

Ours for the Making:
Trans Lit, Trans Poetics
(2011)

IN FEBRUARY 2011, Cheryl Morgan published an essay entitled, "Is There, or Should There Be, Such a Thing as 'Trans Lit'?"

As Morgan points out, there *is* such a thing as "Gay and Lesbian Literature": "Go into a large, urban bookstore," she writes, "and you are likely to find a few racks full of books written by gay and lesbian authors, with gay and lesbian protagonists, aimed at gay and lesbian readers." "Gay and Lesbian Literature" is also alive and well in colleges and universities, where courses, theses, dissertations and sometimes whole courses of study are devoted to it. The term "Gay and Lesbian Literature" attracts readers to bookshelves, students to classes, and scholars to research topics.

In short, "Gay and Lesbian Literature" has made it: in the real world of dollars and cents, marketing strategies, course enrollments and tenure decisions, the term "Gay and Lesbian Literature" has legs.

These days, any American minority can achieve this kind of literary recognition by fulfilling the criteria that Gay and Lesbian Literature began to fulfill a couple of decades ago: lots of authors, lots of books, and lots of readers, students and scholars who expect to find those books grouped together. But although any minority could fulfill those criteria, most minorities haven't. That's why there aren't Serbian-American or Inuit literature sections in Barnes & Noble—and that's why there isn't yet, and might never be, a trans literature section. There are too few trans-identified authors publishing too few books, and too few readers, students and scholars interested in reading, studying and teaching them for "Trans Literature" to be a viable commercial or academic category.

The one arguable exception is trans memoir, by the far the most popular and populous genre of trans writing, and the only one to achieve best-seller status. But most trans memoirs aren't written or read as literature, and far from being established as a viable genre, presses I've contacted claim that there are already "too many" of them (this is a direct quote and oft-repeated rationale) for new trans memoirs to sell.

So, by the standards of the publishing industry and academia, there is no such thing as "Trans Literature." And based on demographics alone, "Trans Literature" isn't likely to be a viable category any time soon. Gay and lesbian people are a minority; transgender people are a hyperminority, and transsexuals—the only sort of transgender people to yet achieve pop cultural recognition (and thus to be able to sell books and fill classes)—make up a small sliver of those who identify as transgender. Unless an improbably high proportion of trans people get busy writing and publishing literature, there won't be much (other than memoirs) to put on "Trans Lit" bookshelves and syllabi in the near future. Even the trans-friendly Lambda Literary Awards tacitly acknowledge the lack of a viable "Trans Literature" category by lumping all trans-related books—academic studies, memoirs, novels, anthologies, poetry, etc.—under a single grab-bag heading.[33]

Morgan argues that if it weren't for publishing-world prejudice, there would be more trans lit, by which she seems to mean fiction by trans authors featuring trans characters. That may well be true. But I'm not ready to equate "Trans Literature" with fiction by and about trans people. For one thing, fiction by and about trans people isn't necessarily literary; I've written a number of stories featuring trans characters, and none were ambitious, interesting, or serious enough to qualify as literature. And what about fiction by trans authors that doesn't feature trans characters—or fiction by non-trans authors that features trans characters? Should either, or both, of these kinds of fiction be considered "Trans Literature"? How about poetry by trans poets that doesn't and poetry by non-trans poets that does directly address trans experiences? And where do trans memoirs fit in—are they all "Trans Literature," or do they also have to be literary to qualify?

These kinds of questions aren't specific to "Trans Literature." Problems of blurred boundaries and contradictory definitions arise with respect to every category of literature. But for the purposes of this essay, let me make things simple, and define "Trans Literature" as literary writing that reflects some aspect of transgender experience.

Like Morgan, most of us look to the demographics of the author and subject matter in order to decide whether literature "reflects some aspect of transgender experience." That's fine when all the demographics line up; a literary novel by a trans author about a trans character dealing with the consequences of gender transition should certainly qualify as "Trans Literature." But as I suggest above, the demographics of author and subject matter often don't line up. The world's most famous trans author, Jan Morris, made a career of travel writing—before and after transition. And as Morgan points out, many of the early twenty-first century novels that feature trans characters are written by non-trans authors.

As a poet, I'm quite touchy about categorizing literature based on subject matter. The commercial publishing world, of course, doesn't bother with poetry, but even teachers and scholars of minority literatures tend to focus more on fiction in which the demographics of author and subject matter align and overlook poetry that doesn't have demographically defined subject matter. Even the poetry of Sappho of Lesbos—the woman-loving lyricist celebrated by ancient Greeks as "the Tenth Muse" whose fame led to gay women being called "Lesbians"—is not always clearly or necessarily lesbian. Some of Sappho's love poems directly address women, but many of her first-person lyrics—like most of the lyric poems written over the past couple of millennia—don't specify the demographics of their speakers. The free-floating, associative "I" of lyric poetry is often not defined in social terms at all—in many lyric poems, the speakers could be male or female, trans- or cisgender, old or young, rich or poor, ethnic majority or minority.

Ironically, the freedom that lyric poetry offers from socially defined identity makes it perfect for trans poets whose sense of ourselves doesn't fit established categories. That's certainly how I saw it during my decades as a closeted trans poet. Lyric poetry enabled me to express myself personally and publicly without either pretending to be male or outing myself as trans. The poems I wrote during these decades are not "about" being trans; the last thing I wanted was to give myself away through explicitly trans subject matter, imagery or metaphors. But by avoiding gender so scrupulously, these poems do reflect an aspect of trans experience—the stigma-driven need to hide or disguise some of the most important parts of one's identity, desires, life.

For example, though I wanted to write sensual, overflowing, Walt-Whitman-having-a-one-night-stand-with-Pablo-Neruda kinds of poems, I couldn't. When I lived as a male, I rarely felt that I had a body, so I drew a blank when I tried to evoke sounds and smells, colors and shapes and textures. I could use the words, I could imitate others' imagery, but because I had never tasted the thrill of living in a body that felt like mine, my poems, despite my efforts, tended to be abstract, intellectual. When I wrote with more feeling, I did so through explicitly fictional personas, writing in the voices of characters I wasn't in order to distance myself from what they were describing.[34]

Since I wrote and published the poems in my first two collections as a heterosexual man, neither my demographics nor my subject matter would qualify them as "Trans Literature." But every sentence, every word, reflected my acute awareness of being trans: my effort to escape gender categories, to avoid revealing personal details, to compensate for my lack of sensual experience through disembodied abstractions, to speak of real feelings through masks that kept me hidden.

So when Morgan asks if there should be such a thing as "Trans Literature," my answer is a qualified yes, because I don't see much aesthetic or intellectual value in a "Trans Literature" that is defined solely by the demographics of author or content.

For "Trans Lit" to achieve aesthetic and intellectual vitality as a literary category, it must be both broader and more ambitious: "Trans Lit" should include all literary texts whose form or content reflects the puzzles, problems, exigencies and insights characteristic of transgender experience—whether or not those texts are written by trans-identified authors or feature identifiably trans characters or content.

For example, the first "trans lit" I encountered—literature that spoke to some experience of being transgender—was Franz Kafka's famous story "Metamorphosis," in which the fabulously unimaginative Gregor Samsa wakes up to find himself transformed into an enormous insect. Though I've never heard any suggestion that Kafka was trans, I've never read a more compelling description of what it feels like to be trapped in the wrong body. But it isn't only the content that leads me to read "Metamorphosis" as "Trans Literature." Kafka's extraordinary use of indirect discourse places us both inside and outside Gregor Samsa's experience, creating a hideously intimate (we have no choice but know how Samsa feels) yet profoundly abstracted narrative perspective that closely resembles the way I experienced my body and my life when I was living as a man.

Yes, I know: after demanding a definition of "Trans Literature" that can apply to lyric poetry, I too turned to fiction for my first example—and for the same reasons that others do. Fiction is a natural mode for representing transgender experience, because many aspects of gender are social and, unlike lyric poetry, in which we hear only individual, private voices, most fiction represents people not only from the inside but from the outside, in relation to one another. "Metamorphosis" shows us both how Gregor Samsa feels *and* how others relate to him, so that we experience, as many trans people do, the tragic mismatch between how others see him and how he sees himself.

For most non-trans people, gender identification—the private sense of seeing themselves as male or female—reflects a sense of consonance between their psyches, their bodies, and the way others identify them. Though the alignment of body, psyche, and social role is always complicated and never friction-free, our language makes it very easy to for non-trans people to express, because it is designed to fit this often-unconscious relation to binary gender.

But there are no terms that readily express transgender identity. Many trans people have fluid, fractured, compound or deliberately paradoxical gender identities; even for a garden-variety transsexual like me, who is simply trying to move from one side of the gender binary to the other, it can be hard to say "I am female" or "I am a woman," because "female" and "woman" imply things about history, socialization, and biology that will never apply to me. The affirmation "I am a feminized genetically male person living as a woman" is not the stuff that stable gender identities and resonant literature are made of.

And for me, as for many trans people, the problem of gender identity goes far beyond a lack of nouns. The blanks in language where words for our gender identities should be reflect deeper blanks in culture, psychology, theology, metaphysics. Without gender identities that comprehend, and enable others to comprehend, the relation between our psyches, bodies and social presence, it can be hard to locate ourselves in relation to space, to time, to nature, to culture, to history, to God.

When it comes to this aspect of transgender experience, poetry, not fiction, is the natural medium. Poetry translates existential experience—including experience for which we have no words—into linguistic form, sound and texture. That makes it a perfect mode for expressing, however indirectly, unstable, contradictory, inexpressible or profoundly uncomfortable gender identities—as long as we have a definition of Trans Lit that finds trans content not just in demographics and subject matter but in syntax, word choice, and other qualities of language.

But how can poetic language reflect trans experience when the subject matter of the poem doesn't? Let me conclude with a brief personal example. While *Transmigration*, the first book I published as a trans woman, directly addresses trans experience, *Psalms*, the book that followed it, doesn't.

Psalms is a collection of lyric poems in which a demographically sketchy "I" complains to God. Though a few lines and images explicitly refer to trans experience, for the most part, I tried to use language that could apply to anyone having relationship problems with the Almighty. But I couldn't escape the fact that my problems with God had everything to do with being trans, and as I wrote, I found that my unstable gender identity—I was acutely conscious of becoming, rather than being, a woman—directly affected my poetic choices. I fudged and frequently reversed my grammatical subjects and objects, and I stretched my sentences over many lines, breaking them into short phrases whose sense kept shifting as one line gave way to the next. I soon realized that the kind of sentences I was writing weren't really sentences, in the sense of syntactically unified, coherent utterances; they were cascades of partial, temporary, transitory meanings, as you can see in this short excerpt from psalm I:9:

> ...Yes, I understand
> Your silence in the face of a woman
> You cannot face

Because you have erased her
Attempts to find some shape,
Some constellation,

In your glimmering syllables of pain
That seem to ask her
Nothing.

At the end of the first line, the focus is on the speaker, but that focus is wrenched by the second line, which in the guise of explaining what it is about "you" (God) that the speaker understands, turns into a description of what appears to be a standoff between them in which God is staring silently at the speaker whom God sees only as "the face of a woman." The third line obliterates this scene by telling us that what the speaker understands is that God *can't* face the speaker, an inability the fourth line seems to explain as a consequence of God's erasure of her. But the fifth line pulls the rug out from under this interpretation by specifying that what God has erased is not the speaker but the speaker's efforts to "find some shape" in something which, two lines later, turns out to be God's "glimmering syllables of pain." This revelation is immediately complicated by the next line, which suggests that these syllables appear to constitute God asking her something, a suggestion that is reversed—erased—by the last line, which tells us they "ask her [the speaker God sees as a woman]/nothing." At the end of this sentence—which is only part of the poem—it is impossible to determine what the speaker understands about God or the relation between them. Like me, the sentences in *Psalms* are publicly, permanently in transition, constantly unfolding the truth they attempt to embody.

I don't mean to suggest that trans poetry "should" be written this way (I don't even write this way anymore). "Trans Literature" doesn't yet exist as a functional cultural category. We've barely begun to name or reflect on transgender experience, or how that experience can be reflected or translated into literature. But though I don't yet know what "Trans Literature" means, I believe that it should mean more than stories by and about transgender people, that "Trans Literature" should embrace any literary language, form, aesthetics or meaning-making mode that reflects transgender experience. By casting the net of "Trans Literature" wide, we will ensure that we are using that category to explore the depth and breadth and formal and existential creativity of transgender experience, to name and describe and lament and celebrate it, and we will recognize that transgender experience is more than the travails of a hyperminority—that it is a particularly striking enactment of a mismatch between psyche, body and social role that is central to being human.

I can't begin to define such a "Trans Literature," but I believe that transgender authors are starting to create it, that non-trans authors like Kafka will one day be recognized as having already created it, and that those who care about queer identity and literature will recognize it, nurture it, cherish it, and come, in bookstores and college courses, to demand it.

Trans Poetics
Manifesto
(2013)

TRANS POETICS are ways of making language do what language is not designed to do: express the unstable relations between body and soul, social self and psyche, which are endured and exulted in by those who don't fit the existing terms of gender and identity. Trans poetics are simultaneously universal—no soul precisely fits a body, no society precisely fits a self, and no self precisely fits the terms available to express it—and unique. Trans poetics enable human beings to express what overflows and is erased by self-defining categories, what melts them, mocks them, fuses and scatters them, recombines them like strands of DNA, waves goodbye to them, falls between their cracks.

Trans poetics aren't defined by demographics. Trans poets write poems that don't use trans poetics, and non-trans poets write poems that do. It doesn't take a carpenter to hammer a nail. It doesn't take a trans person to sing, sigh, scream or psalm the friction between body and soul. Trans poetics aren't intellectual property, a badge of honor, compensation for oppression, an inversion of the gender privilege system, the gender equivalent of Masonic mysteries or a secret handshake.

Like all poetics, trans poetics are partly fantasy. They only exist when we see them, and we only see them when we need to.

Like all poetics, trans poetics may be consciously conjured or recognized in retrospect. (At this very moment, some grad student is probably discovering trans poetics in Homer, hidden like Patroclus in Achilles' armor.)

"Trans poetics" may be unheard of, outlandish, shocking—or they may be familiar poetic means deployed for trans poetic ends. Think of rhyme: the use of sound to call attention to likeness in unlikeness, the revelation that different semantic bodies harbor the same sensuous soul.

Like modernist poetics (remember those?), trans poetics transform meaning from a product provided by the poet into processes within the reader. Like post-modernist poetics (remember those?), trans poetics transform semantic processes within the reader into self-reflexive reflections on the lust for and impossibility of meaning, knowing, being.

Trans poetics show us who we are by showing us who we aren't. Trans poetics show us that who we are *is* who we aren't, and that who we aren't is who we are. Trans poetics transform self-estrangement into self-discovery, self-discovery into the discovery that there is no self, the impossibility of self into affirmation, exposition, industrial revolution, a massive conspiracy, a door, a window, a wrinkle in time, a sob on tiptoe, a song that is singing us.

If we are smart, honest, work hard and stay on our toes, trans poetics will grow through us from yet another fashionably vague critical term into an understanding of language, form, and humanness as precise as a scalpel and as urgent as the silence of God.

Supposed Persons:
Emily Dickinson and "I"
(2013)

I MADE MY WAY ACROSS the frozen lawn of The Emily Dickinson Homestead, crossed the street to the Amherst Women's Club and squeezed myself into one of the last seats left in a large oval of people who braved the bitter January cold to explore the shortest, most frequently used and most important word in Dickinson's poetic lexicon: "I."

I had solid academic reasons for planning a discussion on this subject. The "I" in Dickinson's poems seems both utterly idiosyncratic and uncomfortably familiar (few of us introduce ourselves, as one of Dickinson's speakers does, by saying "I am alive—I guess," but many of us have muttered something like it to ourselves). Her "I" is simultaneously a self-abasing "Nobody" and a confident exemplar of Shelley's vision of poet as "legislator of reality," effortlessly inverting, subverting and rewriting the terms of life, death, soul, God, and eternity.

But I also had a personal stake in this subject. I hoped that our exploration of Dickinson's first-person pronoun would teach me what I meant, what I could mean, by mine.

When I first led an Emily Dickinson Museum Poetry Discussion Group session, my first-person pronouns referred to "Jay," a male persona I created to hide my female gender identity. My "I" referred to someone I both was and wasn't, to a body and biography that never felt like mine. My "I" also referred to the ironic consciousness hiding behind and pulling the strings of my male persona. This binary "I" was remarkably stable—I lived that way for decades—but my two "I"s whirled around one another in irresolvable cycles of self-doubt. Was I my lived male persona, or my unlived gender female identity, or, perhaps, the whirl of doubt, the consciousness of my inability to establish a unitary sense of self?

Now that I live as a woman, my "I" refers neither to a persona nor to ironic distance but to me, Joy, my true self. But as I was reminded during pre-discussion chitchat, it's still not clear what it means when

I say "I." One discussion group member, who'd taken a class I taught years ago as a man, introduced herself as though we'd never met. I didn't explain. Even I'm not sure how "I" can signify both my life as a woman and my life as a man, whether the supposedly unitary female "I" I presented to her conceals, reconciles, or heightens the contradiction between my past persona and present self. My "I" doesn't represent a fixed conjunction of biology, biography, and consciousness, but an ongoing process of self-definition. That sounds marvelously post-modern, but I'd be much more comfortable if I knew more about what, or perhaps how, my "I" means.

Whatever existential wildernesses I wander, I count on Dickinson to have been there and done that, to have written poems that provide pungent, precise language for what seems to me unspeakably confusing and mysterious. I don't think Dickinson was transgender, but the speakers in her poems, like many trans people, tend to locate themselves along margins and boundaries—at home while everyone else is in church, dying while everyone else is alive, bemusedly embarking on the interminable carriage-ride toward "Immortality." Rather than withdrawing because they don't fit the usual social slots, Dickinson's marginal speakers plant themselves at the center of our attention, forcing us to step outside our accustomed perspectives to make sense of what they tell us about their lives.

I wanted to learn to say "I" like that, but couldn't see how to translate the power of Dickinson's poetic "I" into practical strategies of self-articulation. It would have been socially and pedagogically disastrous to explain to my former student that she had indeed met me before, when I was afraid to own a body and afraid to own my soul, when my life had stood in corners like a loaded gun. But Dickinson's speakers introduce themselves in these very terms, and somehow persuade us to try to figure out what they mean by "I" rather than imposing our usual assumptions upon them.

I decided to begin the class by examining Dickinson's own explanation of what "I" in her poems means. In her July 1862 letter to Thomas Wentworth Higginson, she writes, "When I state myself, as the Representative of the Verse—it does not mean—me—but a supposed person." Dickinson, not otherwise known for "stating" her poetics, seems determined to teach her "Preceptor" to distinguish her poetic "I" from her biographical "I," to dissociate the selves she "supposes" on the page from the living, breathing self that supposed them. It's a dance that teachers and critics have been doing since the heyday of New Criticism—the very heyday that, not coincidentally, relocated Dickinson's poetry from regionalist marginality to the canonical center of American literature. Dickinson's poetic achievement couldn't be recognized until readers learned to forestall the impulse to read her engrossingly idiosyncratic, intimate first-person as biography (there she is, forever pining over lost love, effusing ecstatically in a meadow, staring down a patriarchal God), and respond to it as art.

Of course, that's easier said than done. Whenever I teach Dickinson, my students and I have to learn to map the labyrinths between literary and authorial "I"s. But the Dickinson Museum Poetry Discussion group has been at this for years; participants took it for granted that "I" in Dickinson's poems referred to a "supposed person" rather than Dickinson herself. However, as we examined her statement of this principle, we noticed how peculiar her terms are, how hard it was to pin down what she means by "state myself" and "Representative of the Verse." Like Walt Whitman, Dickinson seemed to be turning the language of democracy into the language of poetics. But does "Representative of the Verse" mean that the "I" in Dickinson's poems is analogous to an elected political representative, as her father had been? If so, what constituency does "I" represent? Does Dickinson's poetic "I," like Whitman's, "contain multitudes," or are her "supposed persons" more specific than that?

As we examined the context in which Dickinson presented her theory, we noticed that though the epistolary "I" through which she "states herself" in the letter is putatively biographical rather than "supposed" or "Representative," it seems to contain, if not multitudes, at least two distinct subject positions: the self-abasing self, who, pathetically grateful for Higginson's instruction, insists "You see my posture is benighted," and the self-aggrandizing self who instructs Higginson on how to read her poems. It was clear that Dickinson wanted Higginson to read "I" in her poetry as signifying "supposed persons" rather than her biographical, epistle- and poem-writing self, but it wasn't clear what kind of self the first-person pronouns in the letter signified, or how Dickinson understood the relationship between her writing self and the supposed selves she was writing.

To explore these questions, I drew our attention to one of Dickinson's most accessible poems, one which translates her theory of a non-biographical poetic "I" into practice:

> I'm Nobody. Who are you?
> Are you—Nobody—too?
> Then there's a pair of us!
> Don't tell! they'd advertise—you know!
>
> How dreary—to be—Somebody!
> How public—like a Frog—
> To tell one's name—the livelong June—
> To an admiring Bog!

As we noticed, the informal contraction "I'm" immediately made us feel close to the speaker. "I'm," our most intimacy-promoting form of self-definition, suggests a speaker who feels comfortable enough with us to introduce themselves with an informal contraction even in the rhetoric-inflating arena of poetry. The word "Nobody" heightens our sense of intimacy, confessing a lack of social status that most of us would try to hide when "stating ourselves" ourselves to a stranger. But though the unguarded "Nobody" makes us feel close to the speaker, "I'm Nobody" (which Dickinson may have borrowed from Homer's tale of Odysseus outsmarting the Cyclops) also erases the speaker's biographical self, turning "I" from a sign of identity into a sign of lack of identity—a lack that the speaker embraces as an identity.

Though I didn't share this with the group, the self-erasing self-definition "I'm Nobody" crystallizes what I meant by "I" when I was living as a man. "I" referred to my consciousness that I had no visible, lived identity, no place in the social order, no way to name myself except by negation ("I'm not a man. Who are you?"). I would never have voiced this self-definition, would never have turned "I'm Nobody" from shamed self-awareness into a declaration of identity.

But the speaker of "I'm Nobody" isn't ashamed of the lack of socially sanctioned identifiers. Far from it. The speaker seems to equate being "Nobody" with being a "Representative" self, a self with which others can identify. The speaker's cheerful abdication of social status is followed by an invitation to whoever is reading the poem ("Who are you? / Are you—Nobody—too?") to join the "I'm Nobody" bandwagon. We all felt the pull of this invitation. By the third line, everyone seemed to have signed onto the speaker's populist campaign to invert the social hierarchy and redefine being "Nobody" as an exclusive social club ("Then there's a pair of us! / Don't tell!") and being "Somebody" as an exercise in public self-humiliation, a sign, as one participant put it, that one is "acting like a frog in heat."

By identifying the self as "Nobody" and severing the link between "I" and social identity, the speaker stages a small-scale coup, establishing a tiny rhetorical state, two quatrains long, that offers citizenship to anyone willing to renounce their identifications with social categories and hierarchies, and snicker at "Somebodies" who continue to cling to them.

As we marveled over "I'm Nobody"'s demonstration of the power of Dickinson's non-biographical poetic "I," I suggested that we compare the poem's "I" with the presumably biographical "I" in Dickinson's letter to Higginson. Like the speaker of the poem, Dickinson in this letter is preoccupied with self-definition and social hierachy: her biographical "I" signifies a literary nobody whose identity as a poet is entirely in the hands of the official literary Somebody she is addressing. As we had discussed, the poem's "I" uses self-definition to invert social hierarchy. In the letter, Dickinson's "I" also redefines the social hierarchy that seems to define her. Sometimes, as in "Preceptor, I shall bring you—obedience," her "I" creates subordinate relationship to her "Preceptor." In other phrases, "I" reverses the see-saw, putting Higginson in his place with lordly rhetoric that borders on condescension: "Perhaps you smile at me. I could not stop for that—My Business is Circumference." Like the "I" in "I'm Nobody," the "I" in the letter "states itself," that is, creates a rhetorical state in which "I"'s passive-aggressive self-definitions define her addressee.

These similarities between the self-proclaimed non-biographical, representative "I" in the poem and supposedly personal, autobiographical

"I" in the letter raised questions. Did they mean that the "I" in the letter which articulates the supposed-person theory is meant to refer to a supposed person? Or does the "I" of the poem point more directly than the letter admits toward the biographical "I" of its author?

To explore this conundrum, I suggested we turn to "I'm 'Wife'," a poem in which "I" clearly signifies a supposed person whose life differs crucially from the famously unmarried Dickinson's:

> I'm 'Wife'—I've finished that—
> That other state—
> I'm Czar—I'm 'Woman' now—
> It's safer so—
>
> How odd the Girl's life looks
> Behind this soft Eclipse—
> I think that Earth feels so
> To folks in Heaven—now—
>
> This being comfort—then—
> That other kind—was pain—
> But why compare?
> I'm 'Wife'! Stop there!

Like "I'm Nobody," "I'm 'Wife'" is a poem of self-definition; both poems begin with the intimacy-engendering contraction "I'm," and in both poems, the second words of self-definition make it clear that what the speakers mean by "I" is more complicated than the rhetorical ease of "I'm" suggests. But as the group immediately noted, while the speaker of "I'm Nobody" delights in being a "Nobody," the quotation marks around "'Wife'" show us that "I" is reluctant to embrace the identity of "Wife" even though, as she says, "Wife" moves her to the top ("I'm Czar—I'm 'Woman' now—") of the female status hierarchy.

Those scare quotes frustrate the process of self-definition, making it impossible for the speaker to fully identify herself as "Wife." But we found that the quotation marks themselves define the speaker, locating her "I" in the liminal space where biographical identifiers such as "Wife" and "Woman" (also pincered between quotation marks) are, or aren't, internalized as self-definitions. The speaker isn't allergic to self-definition *per se*; we noticed that she has no typographically-denoted qualms about the non-biographical, clearly hyperbolic assertion "I'm Czar." But from first line to last, whenever the speaker tries to define herself in the terms by which her society denotes mature female identity, she breaks out in quotation marks.

In "I'm Nobody," the speaker turns a marginalizing social identifier into an exuberant, coalition-building, hierarchy-upending self-definition. In "I'm 'Wife,'" the speaker's inability to either embrace the terms through which her society defines her, or, like the speaker of "I'm Nobody," redefine those terms, strands her in self-doubt and isolation. She is a "supposed person" who isn't willing to acquiesce in the biographically-based suppositions that she is "Wife" and "Woman," a person who sees those suppositions, whatever their social benefits, as misrepresenting the "I" they are supposed to identify.

If the speaker were simply uncomfortable with female identity, we could supply the self-defining word she and her culture lacked: "transgender." But as I pointed out, since she speaks wistfully and without quotation marks of "the Girl's life" in the second stanza, her problem isn't gender identity—it is the problem that all people, trans or not, confront, when socially, biographically apt terms for our identities don't fit our sense of who we are. The speaker of "I'm Nobody" solves this problem by embracing a social identifier that erases the link between "I" and biography. But in "I'm 'Wife,'" Dickinson supposes a person who can't solve the problem, who can't erase, escape or redefine the terms of female identity, only hold them at arm's-length, between quotation marks.

The very biography that made it hard for the speaker to define herself should have made it easy for us to define the difference between her "I" and Dickinson's. The speaker is married; Dickinson was single. The speaker has been elevated to a commanding, "Czar"-like social position; Dickinson lived as an unmarried daughter in her father's house. The speaker feels as distant from "the Girl's life" as "folks in Heaven" feel from life on Earth; Dickinson's recurring presentation of herself in child-like rhetorical poses suggests that for her there was never a decisive break between "the Girl's life" and that of "Woman."

Here, then, is the clear distinction between poetic and biographical "I" that Dickinson decreed in her letter to Higginson. But as we strove to bring this supposed not-Dickinson into focus, we kept running aground on those quotation marks.

As one participant pointed out, putting "'Wife'" in quotation marks constitutes a scorched-earth critique of the term, the social status it denotes, and the gender hierarchy that sustains that status. But as another noted, the speaker herself doesn't seem to be making this critique. She is painfully sincere in her efforts to understand herself as "Wife" and "Woman," and sincerely pained by her failure to fully "state herself" in those terms. In other words, the quotation marks reflect two different perspectives, two different speakers jostling within the first-person pronoun: a supposed "I" who can't figure out what's going wrong in her effort to identify herself as "Wife," and an authorial "I" who holds the term up for satirical inspection by the reader. "I" is both a biographical signifier that points to the life of a imagined married woman, and a non-biographical signifier that points to the actual intellectual perspective of the author.

The longer we discussed these meanings of "I," the harder it became to distinguish clearly between them. The supposed-person "I" shares her author's alienation from socially defined terms for female identity. The authorial "I" shares the supposed person's experience of the tragic inadequacy of those terms, her bitter failure to recognize herself in them.

When we turned to the speaker's emphatic declarations in the last two lines of the poem, the meaning of "I" fractured further. The first stanza's halting, dash-riddled reflections attest to the speaker's internal argument, her struggle to convince herself that the power, or at least protection, that "Wife" confers should overcome her sense that the term doesn't fit her. In the second stanza, this argument dissolves into a dreamy reflection analogizing the speaker's now-ended "Girl's life" to "Earth" remembered by "folks in Heaven." But in the third stanza, internal argument turns into a shouting match, as the speaker's "I" begins to split under the strain of trying to define herself as "Wife":

> This being comfort—then—
> That other kind—was pain—
> But why compare?
> I'm 'Wife'! Stop there!

With "But why compare?," the speaker's inability to define herself by either fully embracing or completely rejecting the identity of "Wife" has fractured her into two competing perspectives. Technically, the poem is still a monologue spoken by a single "supposed person," but in the last line's exclamation points, we heard one voice within the speaker—the voice insisting she accept "Wife" as her identity— attempting to shout down the skeptical, alienated side that continues to question the implications and consequences of being "Wife." As we discussed the end of the poem, we realized that we couldn't tell which voice the "I" in the last line represented. Does the exclamation "I'm 'Wife'!" represent the pro-"Wife" voice's triumph in defining the speaker's identity, despite the hesitation represented by the quotation marks, or the alienated side's triumph in showing that even if the speaker can't escape what one participant called "the life sentence" of wifedom, the speaker will never define herself that way?

But if "I" can simultaneously represent self-definition and rejection of self-definition, what does "I" mean? Not the coherent, univocal identity that many of us, including Dickinson in her instruction to Higginson, "suppose" the first-pronoun represents. In "I'm 'Wife,'" "I" is a microphone tussled over by competing definitions of self: "I'm Wife—that's how others see me, and that's how I see myself"; "I might as well be Wife—that's how others see me, that's the role I play and those are the privileges I enjoy, and 'it's safer so'"; "No matter how biography and social status define me, I will never define myself as 'Wife.'" This "I" represents not a self but an ongoing struggle for self-definition that can never be resolved because there are no terms that enable the speaker to whole-heartedly complete the sentence "I'm . . ."

The speaker of "I'm Nobody" avoids this struggle by performing social jujitsu on the term "Nobody," flipping it from a term of denigration into a term of superiority. But to the speaker of "I'm 'Wife,'" the term "'Wife'" doesn't seem denigrating or marginalizing; for reasons she doesn't articulate, the identity of "Wife" simply doesn't fit. As a result, self-fragmenting argument is the closest she can come to self-definition—and only those who recognize that will understand what she means when she says "I."

I understood the moment I first read the poem. I was in my mid-twenties, and had been stuck on the gerbil wheel of frustrated self-definition since childhood. "I'm 'Jay'," I'd say, when I introduced myself. No one heard the quotation marks. No one recognized that the body, biography, and male roles toward which my first-person pronouns pointed weren't what I meant by "I." In fact, until I read Dickinson's poem, I didn't think anyone else knew, or that language could represent, the hell of uncompletable self-definition. Dickinson, I realized, with a rush of gratitude that still brings tears to my eyes, had used the very inadequacy of the language of self-definition to articulate what her speaker and I meant by "I."

As I had throughout the class, I kept my trans perspective on Dickinson to myself. We're still a long way from the time when someone can say "I'm transgender" and expect the sort of response I get when I say "I'm middle-aged" or "I'm Jewish." The discussion wasn't about what my "I" meant; it was about the meaning of "I" in Dickinson.

Several participants were openly disturbed by the self-fragmentation we glimpsed in "I'm 'Wife'." They wondered whether this "supposed person" was an individual case study, or "Representative" of Dickinson's understanding, or even biographical experience, of identity.

It was somewhat reassuring to remember that Dickinson's portrayal of "I" as ongoing process rather than static signifier places her firmly in the line of American thought that stretches back to Emerson and forward to the Pragmatist philosophy and psychology of William James, and that, as we had seen in discussing the letter to Higginson, Dickinson's "I" is akin to Whitman's. But Whitman's "I" is a centrifugal process of expansion through identification; his speakers never complete their self-definitions not because they lack terms with which to identify, but because they identify with every term they can think of. Despite the glad-handing populism of "I'm Nobody"'s speaker, Dickinson is less interested in self-expansion than in the fragmentation that occurs when the language of self-definition fails and selves struggle to "state themselves":

I felt a Cleaving in my Mind—
As if my Brain had split—
I tried to match it—Seam by Seam—
But could not make them fit—

The thought behind, I strove to join
Unto the thought before—
But Sequence ravelled out of Sound
Like Balls—upon a Floor.

The participant who had been most resistant to the idea that Dickinson represents "I" as a self-fragmenting process threw up his hands in surrender when we turned to "I felt a Cleaving in my Mind."

I knew how he felt, and so, I suspect, did Dickinson. For many post-modernist thinkers, and for many transgender people, the idea that identity is, as Dickinson might say, merely "Representative" of an ongoing process of irresolvable fragmentation seems exciting, liberating, a "Get Out of Jail Free" card that guarantees that we will never be limited to the terms of self-definition offered by social conventions, roles, and hierarchies. William James cheerfully rejected the idea that we have unified selves governed by what he mockingly called "the pontifical neuron." Recent studies of the brain and mind support his theory that we all contain multitudes of competing voices, perspectives, and priorities, that selves are not essences but processes of juggling, expressing and suppressing these multitudes, and that our first-person pronouns assert a constant, coherent identity none of us actually have.

But as "I felt a Cleaving" suggests, when Dickinson dramatizes the self in the act of recognizing its failure to define itself, she, like the speaker of "I'm 'Wife'", tends to see it as a crisis—a failure not only of socially provided terms for self-definition but of the very syntax of cognition. We didn't have time to parse the perspectives jostling within the "I" of "I felt a Cleaving in my Mind," either to construe the relationship between the "I" that feels the "Cleaving" and the "Mind" that is being cleft, or to distinguish the self rooted in "Mind" from the self rooted in "Brain" from the self that stands outside "Mind" and

"Brain" and unsuccessfully attempts the phenomenological equivalent of neurosurgery as it tries to "match" the "Seams" along which "Mind" and "Brain" have split. Nor did we manage to do more than speculate about the connection between this speaker's supposed "I" and Dickinson's biographical experience of self-fragmentation. But as we tried to make sense of the gorgeously unravelling final sentence, we noticed that the failure of its "seams" of syntax and metaphor to "fit" mirrored and enacted the very lack of coherence the speaker was describing. In representing the speaker's failed process of self-definition, Dickinson, once again, had fashioned language for an "I" that has no language.

As we pulled on our coats, I thought about what Dickinson had taught me: that I can "state myself" by claiming and redefining terms and syntax that aren't intended to represent selves like mine; that I can use "I" to signify a "Nobody" self that doesn't fit existing terms, roles, and hierarchies; that "I" can represent, can mean, not who I am but my sometimes sputtering processes of self-definition, of becoming. What, I wonder, will I say the next time I introduce myself to someone who doesn't know what I mean when I say, "I'm Joy"?

"Myself—the Term Between":
A Trans Poetic Autobiography
(2015)

WHEN I WAS growing up in the 1960s and 1970s, I would lie awake imagining telling my parents that I wasn't the boy they thought I was, that I was really—

That was where my fantasy conversations foundered. It seemed easy, in my imagination, to tell others what I wasn't, but I didn't know how to explain, even to myself, what kind of human being I was. The only terms I had to describe my oxymoronic combination of female gender identification and male body were those of what we now call "the gender binary," which had no word or place for someone like me. By the time I was old enough to imagine these conversations, I knew without having to think about it that whether someone was male or female (and in a gender binary world, everyone is one or the other) is determined not by who individuals feel we are, but by the sex of our bodies. Binary gender was so widely assumed back then that it had no name—it was just the way things were, the way they were supposed to be. There wasn't even a word for gender as a separate dimension of identity, because in a binary gender world, gender—a sense of identity that often coincides with but is distinct from physical sex—doesn't exist.[35]

There is now widespread awareness of the fact that there are people who don't identify with the sex of our bodies, and there are many more nouns for relations to gender and identity that have no place in binary gender.[36] But useful as they are, nouns are not enough for trans and nonbinary people to express and represent our selves and lives.

This problem—the problem of how to express and represent ways of being human that do not fit widely shared terms, understandings, and conventions—is at the heart of trans poetics. Trans poetics, to me, does not refer to a specific set of representational techniques; it refers to any means we use to address this problem, to express or represent ways of being human that don't fit conventional terms and categories.

"Trans poetics" is a scholarly term developed through analyses of literary representations of trans and nonbinary identities.[37] But to me, as someone whose life has been shaped by the struggle to understand and explain who I am, trans poetics includes all techniques and efforts, literary or otherwise, to express voices, perspectives, and ways of being human that don't fit existing terms of language and culture.[38]

In other words, whether or not we are writers, trans and nonbinary people engage in trans poetics whenever we try to understand, express, or make visible who we are. Those of us who both live and write about trans or nonbinary identities engage in trans poetics on and off the page.

There is a growing body of writing about trans and nonbinary art and lives. But I am not aware of other efforts which, like this essay, try to describe how a trans or nonbinary writer's literary trans poetics reflects the trans poetics of their lives. This essay is barely a beginning to that endeavor, written at relatively early stages in my understanding of gender and in my life as an openly trans poet. But I hope that it will inspire others' explorations into the relations between poems by trans and nonbinary poets and the lives that birth them.

I. ALTERNATIVES TO HONESTY

I started writing what I considered poetry as soon as I learned to write. I don't know why. Poetry wasn't read in my family, and no one knew what to make of the "poems," or rather, rhyming couplets and quatrains, I insisted on showing them. Like my sense that I was female, writing poetry made me different in ways others couldn't understand. But unlike my female gender identification, I wasn't ashamed, afraid of, or willing to hide this difference. Writing poetry was the only activity that seemed to free me from my body and the maleness that went with it; while I wrote, I felt like I was soaring above them, creating a world in which I didn't have to hide, a world that couldn't exist without me.

When I was very young, I didn't care what my poems said, or even if I understood the words I was using. All I cared about was the magic that seemed to happen when I made rhymes, each a brief sense-defying revelation that words that seemed completely different were invisibly but palpably similar. Looking back, I suspect I was so enamored by rhyme because it seemed to enact in sound the revelation I longed for in life: that I, who was apparently so different from the girls around me, was, in some sense-defying way, the same.

If that is true, rhyme was my first attempt at literary trans poetics. But even if it isn't, that childhood writing gave me a way to live outside the world that insisted I, the real me, did not exist. Writing also gave me practice in proudly embracing an aspect of myself that made me different—both key lessons in the art of existential trans poetics.

In junior high school, when I began to attend the first of innumerable writing workshops, I learned that poetry wasn't a strange thing that I and the few dead authors I'd heard of did, but a passion I shared with others, including some who were my age. As I realized that poetry was not just a difference that set me apart, like my hidden gender identification, but something that connected me to others, my idiosyncrasy became an identity: I stopped saying I "wrote poetry," and started saying that I was a poet.

But identifying as a poet—and the workshops and readings that sustained that identity—made me aware of how out of step the poems I wrote were, an awareness that dogged me through my college writing program. The prevailing idea of American poetry—at least the idea that prevailed in the workshops and readings I attended—emphasized poems that spoke plainly, directly, and precisely about personal experiences, feelings, and perceptions. Show, don't tell, I was instructed; use language that sounds the way people do, or at least might, actually speak. Rhyme was an archaic no-no, and so were abstractions and metaphors that did not serve down-to-earth descriptions.

Fine advice for beginning writers. But it wasn't presented as advice. These were not only techniques to learn but norms I had to follow for my poems to be valued. Enforced by the rapid cycles of writing workshop praise and criticism, these norms were directly at odds with the kind of poems I wrote in an effort to express feelings for which there were no words, no images, no colloquialisms, no commonly shared experiences or conventions I could count on others to understand.

My adolescent precursor to trans poetics was as crude and hyperbolic as you might expect: rhyme-stuffed, stress-heavy run-on sentences whose rapidly associated, relentlessly depressive metaphors and abstractions expressed my despair and dissociative distance from existence without so much as hinting at the stifled gender identification that caused them.

It never occurred to me to rebel, to insisting on writing poems in ways that felt true to me. Long before I learned to write, I learned to squeeze myself into the closet of gender norms, to talk and act and pretend to feel the way others believed I should. It didn't take me long to squeeze my writing into the closet of American poetry.

I eliminated rhymes, metaphors, and abstractions, slowed and flattened my rhythms, sprinkled my lines with laboriously colloquial idioms that sounded, my teachers and fellow workshop members agreed, authentic, even though none of us ever used them, and pretended I was writing sincerely about a life in which I experienced and perceived what I would have if my life felt like my life, my body like my body.

No one guessed I was writing fantasy. But the fact that the first-person "I" in my poems referred to someone who didn't really exist made even simple writing exercises ridiculously difficult. Living in a state of dissociation and suicidal depression made it hard to notice the details that are supposed to fill these kinds of poems. Even when describing an object—a favorite workshop assignment—I didn't really see what was in front of me, a difficulty Robert Bly noticed when he visited our high school class and told us to write about the broken branch he placed at the center of the table. I was an abstraction trying to write like a person, a lie imagining what it would say if it were true.

What I learned in these workshops was the opposite of trans poetics. They didn't teach me to how to express a self and life—mine—that language and poetic conventions weren't designed to express. They taught me my self and life had no place in American poetry.

That's why, even though I went to a decade of writing workshops and wrote every day, often for hours at a stretch, it took more than fifteen years for me to complete my first collection, *Alternatives to History*. I started poems all the time, and worked on some for months, but rarely was able to finish any—that is, to make them fit what I then experienced as the contradictory imperatives of art and life, to write poems that simultaneously expressed and erased myself.

Though most of what I was taught about what American poets should do intensified the contradictions that made it hard for me to finish poems, one common workshop exercise gave me a way to finesse them: the persona poem, the practice of writing in the first-person voice of someone or something one clearly isn't. Persona poems are tailor-made for poets who are in the closet. They enable us to be as revealing, honest, and specific as we want about the lives our speakers are describing because those lives, by definition, are not our own.

Ironically, persona poems gave me opportunities to step outside my male persona and imagine what it would be like to a real person, as my fictional speakers believed they were. As long as it was in the voice of someone everyone one knew I wasn't, I could write as though I was trying to tell the truth about about myself instead of working hard not to.

My efforts to imaginatively live through personae, sometimes for months at a time, taught me a lot about developing characters, but it also limited the lives I could imagine these characters living. Though none of the speakers in *Alternatives to History* (or contemporaneously written poems that didn't make it into the book) were transgender, almost all were haunted by a sense of futility, a sense that who they were was painfully at odds with the lives they were living.

The one exception is the persona whose monologues make up the book's concluding sequence, and not coincidentally, that persona, "The Situation," the Israeli euphemism for their interminable and frequently lethal military occupation of Palestinian territory, is the only one doesn't have a body. An abstraction charged with demonic vitality, The Situation whirls effortlessly from perspective to perspective, inhabiting and detonating Jewish and Palestinian bodies with macabre but unquestionable *joie de vivre*.[39] "The Situation" is not about trans identity, but because the persona cannot be understood or represented in terms of gender or other conventional categories, I now see that sequence as my first sustained trans poetic effort—that is, my first effort to express a voice and perspective that defies conventional terms and categories.

But at the time I wrote it (2002), I had no concept of trans poetics and I thought of "The Situation" as an outgrowth of techniques I'd

developed for writing in the closet, an ironically distanced, depersonal-
ized (and thus self-concealing) approach I first encountered in my early
twenties in Eastern European poets—Vasko Popa, Zbigniew Herbert,
and Miroslav Holub—who worked under the vengeful eyes of state
censors. These poets were responding to very different kinds of repression, but their work taught me that the losses entailed by hiding the self
behind the poem—the loss of sensual engagement, the loss of autobiographical richness, the loss of what in an American poetry workshop
would be called "individual voice"—could actually enlarge the scope of
poetry by deflecting attention (both the writer's and the reader's) from
the writer's psyche to general existential conditions. Most importantly,
they taught me what every artist working in the closet has to learn: how
to use camouflage and concealment for expression and revelation.

But "The Soul Wakes Up on the Wrong Side of the Bed" goes further. Combining distancing techniques learned from eastern European
poetry with Dickinson's tactic of talking about "the Soul" in order to
turn psychological intimacies into phenomenological generalizations,
the poem describes what at the time was the most important aspect of
my transgender experience, my dissociation from my body and the life
that went with it:

> This morning the soul would like to freeze
> Into a chiseled block of marble.
> Male or female, it wouldn't matter,
>
> If only it could settle into a single posture,
> With one gold vein gleaming in the groin
> And a slightly saturnine sneer....
>
> The soul is sick, equally sick,
> Of change and changelessness.
> It wants to stand for what it is—
> Or was, or isn't yet,
> For what it no longer remembers except
>
> In the instant it forgets ... [40]

In the eastern European poems I took as my model (for example, Vasko Popa's poem "Between Games"), this sort of patently ironic indirect discourse is intended to defamiliarize common ways of being. Dickinson's soul poems treat more intimate states (such as the experience of impending death invoked in in "A Solemn thing within the Soul / to feel itself get ripe—") in similar ways, inviting readers to identify their own feelings in her descriptions of "the Soul."

Though my soul poem sounds like it is trying to do the same thing, it actually does the opposite, describing a state of being I thought of as linked to my idiosyncratic experience of repressing my transgender identity as though it would be familiar to anyone with a soul.[41] In other words, my trans poetic strategy was to use these techniques to present what would otherwise be closet-opening confession as in the anonymity-preserving guises of critique (the ironic indirect discourse) and phenomenology. Describing "the soul's" disdainful impatience with its body enabled me to describe my disdainful distance from mine. Describing the soul's general, genderless sickness over "change and changelessness" was an attempt to name my excruciatingly gendered state of existential suspension, my sense that I had never been who I knew I really was, my craving to "stand for"—to stand up for and stand up as—the unlived self I could neither remember nor forget.

"The Soul Wakes Up on the Wrong Side of the Bed" was my first taste of trans poetics, my first conscious effort to use poetic language and conventions designed to express widely shared aspects of human experience to instead express the opposite: what I believed was my singular experience of living outside the categories that normally define humanity, neither embodied nor disembodied, male nor female, of being what Emily Dickinson, referring to a very different kind of existential suspension, calls "the term between."

II. WRITING AS A WOMAN

But while I was trying to build a poetry career as a man, I largely avoided even the veiled trans poetics of "The Soul Wakes Up on the Wrong Side of the Bed," opting in most of *Alternatives to History* for abstraction, distancing and disguise, a fact obliquely acknowledged by the word "alternatives" in the title. I knew others would read the title as referring to the ways the poems invent, fictionalize or reimagine events and lives and thus present what could be considered alternative histories; to me, though, it was an abstracted, distanced, and disguised declaration that the poems were written as alternatives to describing my true personal history.

But despite this elaborate camouflage, I still didn't dare to write in the voice of a woman. Only in a few lines of "Fossilized Happiness," a long poem in the voice of a fictional anthropologist overwhelmed by the loss of his wife, is there anything approaching a female voice.[42] Soliloquizing to a lump of rock he believes is fossilized happiness, he recalls snatches of his dead wife's voice:

> I can almost hear her now:
>
> "Science is desire
>   that's learned to present
> its least-tenable conclusions
>   as logical premises." That
> was the sort of thing she said,
>
> often over wine, often
>   in a whisper
> as she cradled my head . . ."

Other than the pronouns that frame it, there isn't much to mark this voice as female. There isn't even a female body behind it: the woman is dead, her words a spume thrown up by the unreliable sea of her husband's memory. Yet even this multiply-distanced performance felt risky, as though I were claiming a right that wasn't mine: the right to speak in the voice of a woman. That sense of risk sharpened as I realized that the speaker's soliloquy was also a trans elegy, an exercise in ventriloquism that enabled me, through the grieving widower's recollection of his dead wife's voice, to indirectly express my grief over the ongoing death of my female self—and, for the first time, to allow myself to imagine how that self might speak:

She said like all religious men

I thought I'd find the meaning of life
    by rooting among the dead.
What if I have, I countered.

Stop rooting, then, she said . . .

The smart-ass toughness of this voice surprised me. I had never had a girlhood or womanhood through which to embrace, reject, or adapt the conventions of femininity. As a result, though I had always felt female, I couldn't imagine what my own female voice would sound like. I vaguely assumed that a voice marked as female would be soft, full of feeling but always dissolving into the expectations of the audience. But as I realized many years later during gender transition, that sort of yielding, boundary-blurring voice was actually the voice I had developed for my male persona, the voice of accommodation, the voice of someone erasing themselves in order to make others happy. The voice of the woman in "Fossilized Happiness" was completely different: mordant, scathingly honest, unwilling to sacrifice truth for love.

Frankly, it scared me. Not because it revealed who I was—because it revealed who I could be.

None of this involved trans poetics. As eccentric as the speaker and his dead wife are, the characters in "Fossilized Happiness" fit common humanity-defining categories: male and female, husband and wife, anthropologist and philosopher, present and absent, alive and dead. But by the time I finished the first, M.F.A.-thesis version of *Alternatives to History*, I was sure that "Fossilized Happiness" was preparing me for a larger project, for the emergence of a voice, a self, a life, I could not yet imagine.

I got a glimpse of that project a few weeks after I finished the M.F.A. program. I was bored by my poetic subjects, cynical about the tricks I'd mastered to give poems the click and sheen of finish, and worn out by decades of trying to write in ways that were simultaneously true and false, honest and dishonest. One summer evening, I was thinking of how sick I was of how I wrote when I heard a voice ask, "Why don't you write like someone else?"

Like who? I demanded. To my surprise, the voice responded with a name—Anna Asher—and a few biographical specifics: Czechoslovakian, Jewish, teenage concentration camp survivor, writing in the 1950's. When I got home, I dutifully scribbled the information at the top of a clean notebook page. The next morning, I started writing words that weren't mine, a series of short, allusively violent poems that appeared as though of their own accord. Whenever I got stuck, I just wrote something that I, as myself, would neveSSr say. Despite the grisly subject matter—rape, starvation, mass murder—this new form of literary depersonalization gave me a kind of euphoric pleasure. For the first time, I was fearlessly embracing writing in a woman's voice.

The series of lyrics stopped as abruptly as they started. I wasn't ready to hear what Anna had gone through, and I didn't know how to describe, or enable her to describe, it.

It took five years for those lyric fragments to grow into *The Book of Anna*.[43]

I didn't mind the lengthy writing process, because it gave me, for the first time, a safe way to imagine and inhabit a woman's life. Even though I never thought of Anna as an alter ego—as that voice had said, Anna was "someone else," someone who was nothing like me—I knew that in writing *The Book of Anna*, I was practicing opening myself to a woman's life, letting that life grow inside me, and through me, enter the world.

At first, Anna's absolute difference from me was exhilarating. I was using language in ways I never had, shattering my outgrown poetic habits, and inverting my lifelong gender discipline: while working on these poems, I was forbidden to speak as "Jay" and required to speak as a woman.

But Anna was hard to live with. She was smarter than I was, and a better poet; she was afraid of nothing while I was afraid of everything. Anna had no pity, for herself or for anyone else; she wasn't nice, she wasn't kind, and she was contemptuous of those like me who clung to such things. Part paragon and part monster, Anna was more cynical, more bitter, more courageous, more complicated and more interesting than I would ever be.

Though I shared few of her strengths, Anna and I had an important problem in common. Like mine, Anna's trauma-shattered psyche, the perspective she developed in the camps, and the experiences she, and I, were trying to express through poetry didn't fit conventional terms and categories, or, for that matter, literary forms and conventions. In other words, though Anna is not transgender, representing her story, her voice, her way of being human, also required trans poetics.[44]

I didn't think of it that way. To me, the challenges of writing Anna were inseparable from Anna herself; throughout the years-long writing process, I thought of myself as trying to learn who Anna was, what story was she was trying to tell, and how she wanted to tell it. She was the one struggling with how to wrench language and literary conventions so that the story of her concentration-camp adolescence would not implicitly rationalize or moralize the atrocity from which her life had emerged or betray her conviction that ascribing meaning to human existence in general or her existence in particular was obscene.

Despite that conviction, I gradually learned that those first lyrics were fragments of Anna's furious effort to narrate life in a way that would enable her to keep living. As she says in the first of the diary entries which surround the poems, "My muse is rage, not beauty."

My muse—not the muse inspiring my poetry (to me, the muse model of composition seems terminally masculine) but the muse inspiring my attempt to transform gender from a mode of repression into a mode of creation—was Anna. A good muse suffuses the isolated process of writing with the libidinous thrill of a tryst. Thinking about Anna, listening to her voice, stretching my poetics toward hers, certainly thrilled me. But a top-drawer muse doesn't only make writing more fun; she makes it both necessary and possible to do the impossible. Anna enabled and required me to turn stultifyingly circular questions about whether I was or could ever be a woman into much more interesting questions about narrative, language, and poetics—questions about the stories Anna needed to tell, the kinds of words and sentences she needed to tell them, and how the medium of poetry might transfigure the existential, psychological and religious problems that were killing her. The answers—mine and Anna's—sounded like this:

> He lives, I hear, outside Cologne
> in a place that resembles Heaven
> as water resembles glass.
> He lives. I hear, outside
>
> a place that resembles Heaven
> as cologne resembles glass,
>
> the crack of a brass-tipped staff (from "Tamar")[45]

Anna's "He" was a high-ranking SS officer who raped the 14-year-old Anna and, when the resulting pregnancy was brought to his attention, forced her to self-abort with a bedspring, an act that left her sterile. This story had nothing to do with me—I had no personal experience with the Holocaust or rape—but in retrospect it is clear that these scenes resonated with my subjugation by the all-powerful masculinity (the "He" who got to live my life, the man the world called "Jay") that forced me to continually abort the female self with which I was continually pregnant.

As Anna learned to tell the story of her life, I was learning too—not how to tell the story of my life (I still didn't have one), but how to use the materials of my liminal existence to make story out of silence, self out of circumstances that erased it. While those were important baby-steps forward in my arrested development as a person, what mattered most in terms of trans poetics was that, in response to Anna's determination to be written, I had finally begun to develop the insight that flickered in "The Soul Wakes Up on the Wrong Side of the Bed"—the insight that my self-canceling approach to existence could be translated into poetically effective syntax.

Many years before I began *Anna*, former U.S. Poet Laureate Robert Hass planted the book's seeds in a craft lecture about form in poetry delivered at the Napa Valley Writing Conference. According to Hass, form was not a matter of adopting or rejecting a prosodic pattern; it was a reflection and expression of the writer's sense of the shape of life.

By means of illustration, Hass offered the example of a young artist who sculpted smooth, beautifully ovoid sculptures until she suffered a devastating miscarriage that left her sterile; when she found her way back to art, the forms she created were jagged, discordant, unresolved and unresolvable.

It's obvious now that Anna's description of her self-performed abortion directly echoes Hass' linkage between miscarriage, metaphysics, and poetic form. But what struck me when Hass spoke was the poverty of my conception of existence. I could intellectually conceive a variety of shapes—life as a circle, life as a tragedy, life as a joke, life as a stumble or leap toward revelation—but I didn't experience life as having a shape, or, more accurately, I couldn't conceive of my own experience as a microcosm through which I could make sense of life, and so could not shape my poems in ways that would enable anyone else to do so.

As Hass' anecdote suggests, an artist's sense of the shapeliness of existence is less a matter of philosophical reflection than of lived, bodily experience. My experience of life consisted of doing my best not to live, and I experienced my body as a smothering mask—when it didn't feel like a tomb. I didn't want to create poetic forms that would turn my sense of the shape of life into a microcosm; mine wasn't an existence I wanted to propagate. So, as I wrote *Alternatives to History*, I decided to approach poetic forms as experiments, theoretical projections of what life might be if it had this or that shape—in short, to write poems that were alternatives to the history I myself had lived. Alas, as Hass could have told me, neither form nor poetry work like that. Despite my conscious intentions, the poems in *Alternatives to History* reflect my stunted experience of life.

As I worked on *Anna*, I realized that conceptions of the shape of life—William James, in his Pragmatist philosopher mode, calls them "world-formulas"—are not only embodied in the forms of whole poems; they are implied, albeit dimly, by the syntactical form of each sentence.[46] This led to what I would now call a trans poetic breakthrough: the realization that rather than projecting a single, unifying shape of existence, as Hass described, a poem's form could consist of the sentence-by-sentence morphing of one world-formula into another. Of course, a conception of form that magnifies the constant slip and slide of world-formulas makes it hard for a poem to end up projecting a single, stable notion of existence. But to Anna, world-formulas were little better than the lampshades the Nazis made out of human skin. Any means of giving form to the story of her life that implied a unifying shape to existence was simply a screen for the blaze of atrocity.

This new (to me) idea of form produced a radical shift in my approach to syntax. I started thinking of sentences, individually and collectively, as processes of transformation, and when I did so, Anna found herself able to begin to tell the story of her life:

> He lives, I hear, outside Cologne
> in a place that resembles Heaven
>
> as water resembles glass.
> He lives. I hear, outside
>
> a place that resembles Heaven
> as cologne resembles glass,
>
> the crack of a brass-tipped staff. I hear
> he lives, doused with cologne. Cologne
>
> drips from the springs
> in his bed. I hear
>
> spring's brass-tipped staff
> cracking ice that resembles Heaven
>
> as water resembles glass. Cologne
> drips from a ceiling crack.
>
> He lives here, a brass-tipped staff. Sweating
> cologne and shards of glass,
>
> ready to spring,
> I hear Heaven crack. ("Tamar")

The first sentence projects an urbane sense of a life in which details—even details like the location of the mass murderer who raped her—can be noted, mulled, analogized and abstracted. Nothing terrible is going to happen in a world where we can frame such sentences, and even if it does ("He," after all, "lives"), that terrible thing happens far from the Olympian plane from which the speaker regards existence. That world-formula is erased in the terse declarative that follows; there is nothing urbane about the brute fact that "˜He lives." The third sentence repeats but deranges most of the words of the first: in the funhouse-mirror syntax of its first two-and-a-half lines, "I hear" is transformed from easy rhetorical gesture into an urgent present-tense act. But the immediacy and agency of "I hear" is attenuated by the stanza-plus qualifying clause that follows it—a clause that purports to locate the speaker but actually confounds any sense of location (unless we can figure out where the outside of "a place that resembles Heaven / as cologne resembles glass" might be). The analogies of the opening sentence imply a world-formula of above-it-all intellection, but the analogies in this one imply a world in which neither the speaker nor we can define our location—and thus our distance from "him." The direct assertion that concludes the sentence—"the crack of a brass-tipped staff"—once more implies a concrete, knowable world of subjects and objects. But this glimpse of world dangles uneasily at the end of the clauses that precede it. Either the yoking of these discordant world-formulas betrays the unifying promise of syntax—the promise that all parts of a sentence, no matter how complex, do indeed relate and add up to a whole—or syntactical unity requires us to accept the concrete and knowable as a subordinate clause of a world that is neither. By the end of the passage, the distant real-estate of Cologne has become ceiling-soaking cologne, and the distance between "He" and "I" has collapsed with Heaven-cracking violence, a transmogrification that suggests the syntax- and narrative-defying extremes to which Anna's experience has pushed her.

Anyone whose syntax spans this range of order and disorder is having a hard time formulating her world. At the same time, of course, Anna—and I, her phantasmal hanger-on—had made a trans poetic discovery: our inability to formulate the shape of existence could itself be a means of generating poetic form. Neither Anna's traumas nor my lack of a body or self I could call my own doomed us to silence; they were beginnings, not ends.

III. TRANSMIGRATION

By making form and meaning out of a self whose core experiences defied form and meaning Anna, the character, and *Anna*, the book, gave me my first sustained demonstration of literary trans poetics. But that demonstration had not taught me much about trans poetics in life. Before, during, and after *Anna*, I remained a closeted, agonized, something or other who not only shied from expressing my female gender identification but worked day and night to build a life as a man, Jay Ladin, who fathered children, published poems and literary criticism, applied for and occasionally landed a string of teaching positions. *Anna* had been both a channel for my repressed gender energies, and a way of imagining a woman's voice and life without cracking my masculine mask. When I finished the book, I felt bereft, lost as a poet and a person. After five years of writing and vicariously living through Anna, how could I go back to doing nothing on or off the page but pretending to be a man?

By this point, maintaining my male persona was a matter of conscious self-mutilation, a regimen that had become so habitual I didn't notice that it was determining more and more of my existence. Every breakdown in my discipline was immediately followed by the imposition of new rules and strictures. By the time this regimen (and I) fell apart, I had, among other things, forbidden myself to move the sun visor while I was driving, and would only eat or drink when others invited me to.

In short, repressing my gender identity had driven me crazy, turning my existence into an exercise in obsessive-compulsive behavior. Ironically, the justification for my craziness was my fear of losing my grip on what everyone else, I was sure, would consider my sanity: the male identity that matched my male anatomy. According to then-current versions of the Diagnostic and Statistical Manual of Mental Disorders, transsexuality, which had by then been listed under the sanitizing technical monicker "Gender Identity Disorder," is a mental illness.[47] I had never before experienced it that way; my sense of myself as female had always felt like a form of sanity. But as my need to live as who I knew I was became more urgent and intense, so did the savagery of the ways I repressed it—a vicious escalating cycle that was definitely a disorder.

My hysterical commitment to the conventions of gender had stunted my pre-*Anna* poetry, making it hard for me to transgress conventions of diction and syntax, despite my envious awe of poets like Emily Dickinson, who shrugged them aside whenever they impeded their vision. Even after years of studying and writing about Dickinson, I couldn't verb or adjective a noun, misinflect a verb, or do anything that might make my sentences sound "wrong"—and thus might point, however obliquely, toward the wrongness cowering behind the façade of my life.

Though Anna never approaches the linguistic boundary-shattering I admired in Dickinson, she warps syntax, mixes dictions, and generally misbehaves in language more than "Jay Ladin" ever had dared to in "his" own name. But when *Anna* was over, so was my flirtation with poetic transgression—and, I thought, with female identity, until the spring of 2005, when I started dying.

Dying took me by surprise. Having never felt alive, and often contemplated (and occasionally tried) suicide, I felt immune to involuntary forms of mortality. But there my body was, refusing to take in or digest food, refusing to sleep, refusing to do anything that suggested that it, that I, was actually alive. My dissociative détente with my body—our longstanding agreement that I wouldn't kill it if it didn't require me to pay attention to it—had been broken. Nothing could distract me from the fact that I was entombed in flesh that disgusted me.

Without any conscious decision or grand trans poetic gestures, life as I had known it, my outwardly settled life as a married male academic, ended. As the structures, conventions, habits and identities to which I clung shattered or spun away, I was seized with the need to write poetry. But who would I write as? *Anna* was done, and "Jay Ladin" was a nightmare from which I was trying to awake. I began a crash course in trans poetics, because without ways of expressing my excruciating experience of drifting between self- and humanity-defining categories and trying to locate myself among them, there was no way I was going to make it from one life to the next.

HOPE

It may turn out the soul said
That I don't *want* to live

That life is too far away
Too deeply buried

In the future
And the past

It may turn out the soul repeated
That what you call life and I call life

Is not life at all
But a strip of flesh

Ripped without permission
From the body of those

For whom I live
If I live the soul said . . .[48]

Rule number one for a closeted transsexual is not, under any circumstances, to tell the truth about how you feel. Though I hewed to this rule in the conduct in my life, it seemed anathema to do so in poetry, and so, like other closeted writers, I devoted myself to disguising the emotional truths I told—ascribing them to fictional personae, abstracting them into philosophy or metaphysics, twisting them into metaphoric pretzels, anything to avoid doing what this poem does: saying simply, directly, like a child who doesn't know enough to fear the consequences, "I don't *want* to live." This directness was for me a liberatory act, a leap into the unknown world of those who say what they feel. In direct violation of rule number one and every other rule I'd developed to keep myself in male drag, there was finally a direct correspondence between how I felt and what I said.

Of course, I was still distancing myself from the feelings I was expressing by putting them in the voice of "the soul." But as in "The Soul Gets Up on the Wrong Side of the Bed," I couldn't describe a generalized soul without describing my own. Moreover, by ascribing these feelings to "the soul," I was sincerely doing what "The Soul Wakes Up on the Wrong Side of the Bed" only pretended to do: I was staking what for me was the radical claim that I wasn't *sui generis*, something non- or less than human, but a soul like other souls.

By the logic I had followed all my life, the extremity of my experience should have further isolated me from humanity. I'd certainly never known anyone who had gotten caught, as I was caught, in the psychic spin-cycle of death and rebirth. But the poems that were pouring out of me—poems that, like "Hope," spoke with phenomenological sincerity of and for "the soul"—proclaimed the opposite: that the anguish that had pushed me out of hiding connected me to all who struggle toward lives that express and sustain them.

In many ways, the simplicity of "Hope" reflected the simplicity of my existence, trembling between life and death. But that simplified existence was also very complicated. Five people, myself included, depended on my assistant professor's salary—and thus, until I received tenure, on the maintenance of my male persona. At the same time, I needed to spend as much time as possible developing my phantom sense of femaleness into a full-fledged, clothes-wearing, street-walking, phone-answering identity. As I struggled to meet these contradictory imperatives, I found myself constantly switching genders, an inadvertently trans poetic lifestyle (after all, switching genders expressed the fact that I fully fit neither) that I thought of as an uncomfortable stop on the way to fully living as—and, I believed, completely fitting into the binary category of—a woman. I would wake up as myself—as my best approximation of a woman—and stay that way until I approached the school where I taught, at which time, either in a gender-neutral Starbucks bathroom or (once or twice) on the street, I would change back into male drag. I would teach all day as a man, leave school, duck into another bathroom and change back into myself for a couple of hours. When I couldn't walk the streets any more, I had to switch again: I was staying in a youth hostel, and had to look enough like the man on my ID to get in. In short, my early gender transition was a process of constant alternation, of letting my fledgling female self unfold and amputating it again.

Most people who are supportive of transitioning transsexuals are eager to see our lives swing from the negative pole of self-obliteration to the positive pole of selfhood. I was eager to see my life swing that way too. I thought that motion would be as simple as the gender binary itself: living as a man was bad, so living as a woman must be good. To my surprise, once I embarked on the transition process, those simple binaries—male and female, good and bad—vanished. The revolving door of gender I was caught in was lonely, confusing and painful, but for the first time in my life, my gender-related agony reflected hope rather than despair. It was bad that my insistence on my female identity was destroying my marriage, but it was good that I was finally becoming a person rather than a persona—though it was bad that my personhood was so easily and frequently deconstructed.

In short, what was best about my life was indistinguishable from what was worst, and the syntax in much of *Transmigration*, the book that collects "Hope" and other poems I wrote during the death of my male persona and emergence of my female-identified true self, reflect this dizzying, morality-confounding, world-formula:

LOSING YOUR BREASTS

Every night you lose your breasts.
First one and then the other.

Every night one breast falls into an inaccessible place
A crack between you and you

Between the you you were and the you you will be
If you ever find your breast.

There is no sound when it falls.
There is a sound a very soft sound

As you stare into the inaccessible place
Between you-will-be and you-were.

When you look up the other breast is gone.
You have lost yourself yourselves I mean.

No—a breast is not a self.
A self isn't too large and too small

Asymmetrical lumpy the self
Doesn't give milk no matter whose lips are on it

The self isn't tender the self
Is not attached.

Of course neither are your breasts
When you grope for them in the inaccessible place

Between you and the something less
That is you when you lose your breasts,

When they lose themselves like girls
Watching each other disappear

Into the future that opens in the dark
The inaccessible crack

Between the wall
And the bed.[49]

The literary trans poetic strategies through which "Losing My Breasts" expresses my experience of wobbling, whirling and falling between the cracks of maleness and femaleness aren't hard to see. The poem constantly repeats the same few words, arranging and rearranging them in simple declaratives that amplify and extend each other's meanings even as they deflect or flat-out contradict them. "Between you and you" becomes "Between the you you were and the you you will be" which becomes "Between you-will-be and you-were" and then, toward the end, "Between you and the something less." Each iteration is given equal weight, as is every other statement in the poem; none is presented as more or less true, and there is no sense of narrative progression from one to the other. As a result, the basic assertion that there is a measurable, important difference "between you and you" ramifies, becoming a way of thinking about different versions of self ("the you you were and the you you will be"); a distinction between forward- and backward-pointing existential vectors ("you-will-be and you-were"); and a recognition of the constant degradation and reconstitution of self ("Between you and the something less"). All of these are aspects of the peculiar breakdown and recombination of binaries which, I was learning, was an inescapable aspect of gender transition.

As a writer, I found this liminal condition and the poetic tactics it demanded fascinating, but as a person, I couldn't wait to leave it behind for a more stable identity. I wanted to find out who I would be, and how I would write, as a woman.

IV. HALF THE HUMAN RACE

Anna notwithstanding—and Anna certainly doesn't sound like any woman I've ever heard or read—I had spent a lifetime living, speaking and writing as a man. As I contemplated the suddenly imminent prospect of living as a woman, I needed to know whether I could write as myself in a female voice. What, I wondered, made a female voice "authentic"? How did the language used by women differ from the language used by men? Could such language ever seem to me like a natural mode of expression, or would I always feel as though I was writing in someone else's voice when I wrote as a woman?

I decided to find out by writing poems using only words I found in magazines written by and for women. I started with *Woman*, a free newspaper that caught my eye in fall 2006, at the beginning of my last two semesters of teaching as a man. In a procedure I have used ever since, I made lists of evocative words and phrases I noticed as I leafed through the pages. I soon realized that I couldn't forage for language if I read the articles; I needed to scan the words on the page without regard for the units of meaning to which they belonged.

I had no idea what I was trying to say, no sense of what or how or whether the language I was collecting might mean something. I just threw words and phrases together, until, like Rorschach inkblots, I started to recognize shapes in them—strange, shadowy sentences no one was uttering, peculiar metaphors and images arising from unlikely juxtapositions, and then a voice that slowly, through many drafts and revisions, began to sound like it was saying something I needed to say. Began to sound like mine.

This was not, at first, a trans poetic exercise. I didn't set out to express or represent my oxymoronic combination of female gender identification and male life and body, my experience as a transgender person, or the transmigratory betweenness reflected in poems like "Hope" and "Losing My Breasts." I wasn't trying to learn how to write as someone who didn't fit binary gender categories; I was trying to learn—to see if I could learn—how to write as a woman.

I don't think I ever learned to do that, or even whether there is such a thing, apart from writing from the life experience or subject-position of being a woman. But the words I found in *Woman* had taught me that, in English at least, women's vocabularies are infinitely richer in words for color, texture, fabric, feeling and relationship. That wasn't surprising. What was surprising was how few of these words, all of which I knew, and many of which are common among men as well as women, it had ever occurred to me to use in my poems. I knew that my male socialization had discouraged me from using language that was culturally marked as female, but I hadn't realized that my lifelong fear of revealing my female gender identification had turned this predilection into an unconscious inner taboo so powerful that, when writing poems, I didn't even remember these words were available.

I was also surprised by the authority that crackled through the language I found in *Woman* (and later, in other women's magazines). Every article lectured the reader about what the author assumed every woman needed to know, presuming both absolute knowledge of what women ought to do and intimate knowledge of the presumed deficiencies of each reader. I had written a Ph.D. dissertation about the modernist techniques American poets of the early twentieth century developed to compensate for poetry's loss of its nineteenth-century rhetorical and epistemological authority. Every page of the not-particularly-well-written *Woman* spoke with assurance and command Eliot, Pound and company had twisted themselves in knots to approximate. Treating that language as material for my poems was like finding buried treasure in a pile of newspapers.

As I worked *Woman*'s sensuous, emotional, how-to-oriented phrases into poetry, I was amazed by the imaginative energy they released. My poems had always struggled to speak of self and world in terms of emotion, smell, touch, taste and sound. The language I remixed from *Woman* seemed to do all those things more or less automatically:

> ... Disconnected
> from the marriage
>
> that insulated you completely
> from the circle of women,
> it is remarkable to see
>
> the blessing of the feminine
> happening on subtle levels, filling your body
> with gleaming conch shells and brightly colored fruit,
>
> knitting your fears
> into hope for connectedness. Yes darling,
> a life of freedom and comfort
>
> will be served in the Carriage House,
> in an all-girls community
> where fine specimen roses climb
>
> winged poles damaged by trauma,
> while Grandma Pearl taps her feet
> a century apart in pretty, private rooms,

cleaning and energizing
the life you share
with generations of women . . . [50]

This short passage contains a remarkable number of words not culturally marked as female that I'd never considered using in decades
of writing poetry, including "cleaning," "energizing," "trauma," "community," and "subtle," among others. Life in the trans closet had not
only cut me off from words like "knitting," but from vast swathes of
diction—and thus cut my imagination off from much of what it means
to be human. My inability to think of these words as poetic material—
and the inability of my poems to address the experiences and perspectives to which they speak—was not a direct result of being trans; it
was a consequence of the reflexive self-policing and self-amputation
through which I kept myself within the boundaries of masculinity.
As the *Woman* poems began to take shape, I realized how carefully I
had avoided words that might lead to too-precise (and thus potentially
self-revealing) articulation of psyche or feeling. For example, in innumerable poems about isolation, I had never allowed myself to speak
directly about being "disconnected" or "insulated." As I cut myself
down to fit the Procrustean bed of masculinity, I had no idea what
limbs I was losing in the process.

At first I thought of these "magazine poems"—that's what I called
them—as collages of cut-up text, but I soon realized that there was a
better artistic metaphor. I was using *Woman* as a lexical palette, blend-
ing, layering and spattering its diction like an expressionist painter.
By what seemed to me an odd coincidence—I had never thought
academia would teach me anything about poetry—I had studied a
theory that made sense of this approach some years before, when,
while completing a Ph.D. and working on *Anna*, I was introduced to
mid-twentieth-century Russian thinker Mikhail Bakhtin's *The Dialogic
Imagination*.[51] Bakhtin's claims about poetry alternately angered and
amused me, but what he said about the social and ontological dimensions of language taught me to think precisely about aspects of writing that had always seemed vague and mysterious. Bakhtin points out
that a language is not a homogenous medium, but a "heteroglossic"

(his term—literally, "many-tongued") constellation of dictions, each deriving from and pointing toward different perspectives, values, areas of experience. My writing workshop training had taught me to minimize the heteroglossic aspects of language, to subordinate them to a single homogenous poetic "voice," an effect that Bakhtin terms "monoglossia." Bakhtin's descriptions of monoglossia as a willful sublimation of the heteroglossic richness of language opened my eyes to all I had lost by smoothing over the differences between words and the world-formulas they reflected in poems. He enabled me to recognize that my character Anna's voice had to be heteroglossic, because her concentration camp experiences had gutted her belief in the individual world-formulas implied by specific forms of diction. By the same token, I had always worked earnestly toward monoglossia in poems I wrote as "Jay," because monoglossia made it easier to minimize potentially revealing connotation, contradiction, and other things that might give me, the closeted trans me, away.

Now my male persona was crumbling, and the heteroglossic flood of forbidden dictions I found in *Woman* and other women's magazines seemed to express the tide of long-suppressed vitality that persona had kept in check. As these dictions gathered into a new heteroglossic mode of expression, the voice they formed was not the personal female voice I had hoped to discover, but a louder, impersonal, archetypal voice, a voice in which the how-to authority of women's magazines became a mode of prophecy whose social, psychological, and political breadth ("an all-girls community / where fine specimen roses climb / winged poles damaged by trauma") was inseparable from its intrusive intimacy ("knitting your fears / into hope for connectedness").

My initial goal of "writing as a woman"—the literary equivalent of the passing I saw as the goal of gender transition—didn't require trans poetics; it was not an attempt to be human in a way that defied conventional categories, it was an attempt to fit my humanity into and express myself through through those categories.

This voice was a different matter. This was not the voice of "being a woman," not the voice of neatly demarcated identities, roles and behaviors. This was a volcanic language of becoming, critical and affirming, penetrating and tender, ruthless in its diagnoses and uncompromising in its insistence that "you"—I—embrace the maelstrom that is real, embodied life. Human categories couldn't define or contain this voice, a voice demanding that after a lifetime of doing the opposite I become fully, unapologetically alive.

That is the goal of gender transition.

But I didn't know that then. I hadn't yet tried to fit myself into conventions of female gender expression, hadn't yet learned that after a lifetime of hiding, cringing, lying, and dying, I couldn't do anything that would make me less than who and what I knew myself to be.

So while I was harvesting their diction, I read the articles in *Woman* and its glossier cohorts, hoping to learn what I had to do, and have, and get, and want, and feel to really be a woman. I never learned much about that. What they taught me was that being a woman does not mean serenely embodying an unchanging platonic essence; it is a process of learning and growing, trial and failure, self-doubt and reinvention. In fact, from a women's magazine perspective, being a woman seemed a lot like being a transsexual in transition, a constant battle to transform biological givens, such as the ease with which female bodies store fat, and adverse social interpretations of those givens, such as the constant pressure to measure ourselves against Photoshop- and bulimia-perfected "models," into self-actualizing self-expression.

Though I hoped that the generalized language of poems like "Hope" would speak to a wide audience, I had feared that writing about gender transition would ghettoize my work, aim it irrevocably toward a hyperspecialized, infinitesimal coterie of poetry-reading transsexuals. Women's magazines were trying to teach me that non-trans women also struggle to become themselves. Many years later, when I had outgrown trying to "act like a woman" and had grown into myself, I realized that no one really, perfectly fits the categories through which human beings define one another and ourselves. That means all of us need trans poetics to understand and express all of who we are.

V. INCONCLUSIVE CONCLUSION (2015)

I don't mean this to be an authoritative or prescriptive account of trans poetics in poetry or in life. Every trans and nonbinary person undergoes different crises and achieves different triumphs; each collision between the processes of becoming and the processes of poetry will produce different imperatives, frustrations, discoveries.

But the relationship between the ways I have experienced being a person who doesn't fit binary gender categories and the trans poetic tactics I developed to express them suggests that exploring the intersections between trans lives and trans art has much to teach us all about what it means to be creatures whose selves are shaped by the ways we express them.

Trans poetics aside, I have learned that poetry is a way of being alive, a way of being more alive, a way of living beyond our lives. Because I kept writing, I kept living; I was not an end in myself, but a means for poems to be written. To me, this truth—that poets exist so that poems can be written—seems self-evident. My life, even when it wasn't a life but a deathly impersonation of one, continued, because I lived through the poetry that came to life through me. The need to write poetry, to write the poems that needed me to write them, was far from the only drive that pushed me toward gender transition, but it was the drive that kept me going when everything else that gave me meaning or direction seemed to have vanished. The thread I followed through the labyrinth of becoming, the only thread that remained unbroken, was poetry.

Writing Beyond the Human:
Divining the Poetics of Divinity
(2020)

MY JOB AS A POET these days is to give voice to the Shekhinah, who, in Jewish tradition, is the female, immanent aspect of God, present in human lives and sharing our sufferings.

Conveying divine voices in human language is one of poetry's most ancient functions. But though I've often written to or about God, before I embarked on this project I had never tried to write poems through which divinity would speak.

The Shekhinah isn't just divinity; the Shekhinah is divinity in the key of she, divinity conceived as female. Like most people I know, I grew up in a world in which everyone, believers and non-believers alike, imagined God as male. In prayer books, Bibles, sermons, and conversations with Jehovah's Witnesses who occasionally rang our ethnically Jewish doorbell, God was always "He." Even atheists referred to God as male: "What evidence do you have that He exists?" they would ask, or, if they were particularly pugnacious, "If God can do anything, can He create a weight that He cannot lift?"

I never thought of God as male, or gendered at all. As someone born male but who from early childhood identified as female, I knew from personal experience that gender does a painfully poor job of relating bodies and souls. I couldn't imagine why a divine being who had no body would bother with gender at all.

But though I didn't conceive of divinity in terms of gender, I was drawn to the idea of the Shekhinah from the moment I came across it, not as theology, but as an image of female identity independent of a female body. Everyone I knew assumed that gender identity (whether someone considers themselves male or female) was determined by physical sex, an assumption that meant it was inconceivable for someone like me to exist. But no one questions whether the Shekhinah is female. The most conservative religious authorities and the most trans-skeptical Jewish feminists—people who would never accept my female gender identification—embrace the Shekhinah as "She," though she is no more physically or socially qualified for that pronoun than I am.

That was the way the Shekhinah first found her way into my poetry: not as a form of divinity but as a closeted code for transgender identity, a way to refer to my disembodied sense of femaleness without blowing my cover as a heterosexual man. For example, one of the poems in my first collection presents the eponymous Shekhinah as an invisible female presence whose most perceptible manifestation is a perfume-scented breeze. In that poem, as in my life at the time, this presence has little power beyond persistence. The world she perfumes has no place for her and is beyond her ability to change.

Ten years later, when I had realized I could no longer live as a man but hadn't yet decided whether that meant suicide or gender transition, a much more active and disruptive version of this presence, which I referred to only as "she," appeared in a poem called "Following the Script." "She" had no interest in wafting invisibly through the world or in perfuming my lifeless life; instead, she summons, prods and pushes the reluctant second-person subject of the poem to embark on the family-shattering process of gender transition "you" keeps trying to avoid. She was successful. When I began the poem, I was living as a man; two years later, I was living as myself.

Even in this more potent form, my poetic Shekhinah was a secular, not a theological, figure, a metaphor for my now-irrepressible female gender identification rather than a manifestation of divinity. As Eric Selinger, in his delightful essay "Shekhinah in America," points out, Jewish American poets had long treated the Shekhinah in a secularized way. Selinger traces the practice to Jerome Rothenberg, who included the Shekhinah among the materials from Jewish tradition he repurposed for mid-twentieth century poetry, and cautioned those who might do the same that "The Shekhinah's 'reappearance among us is an event of contemporary poesis, not religion.'"[52] As Selinger explains, other Jewish American poets

> follow[ed] Rothenberg's lead in linking the Shekhinah to *poesis*, the broad Latin term (from the Greek *poiein*) for the creation and shaping of poems. Norman Finkelstein

and Maeera Shreiber call her, respectively, the "mistress of presence and absence, immanence and transcendence" (93) who serves as the "founding figure of Jewish poetic making"; while the poet Allen Grossman declares that "it is for knowledge of her that the people should look to the Jewish poet and the Jewish poet to his or her own nature."[53]

I wasn't aware of this tradition; I absorbed it by osmosis. My modern American poetic upbringing trained me to think of poems as inherently secular, and to think of *poesis* as a process that, because it secularizes everything included in a poem, automatically turns the Shekhinah into a sign or symbol of something else, of "presence and absence," or female gender identification—anything but divinity.

Unbeknownst to me, some other Jewish American poets—particularly those re-imagining Jewish tradition from feminist perspectives—rejected both the Shekhinah's secularization and the binary cleavage between *poesis* and religion. In their works, the Shekhinah is not just poetic material; she is a vital, divine female presence who, as we see in Alicia Ostriker's well-known "A Prayer to the Shekhinah," counters the spiritually stunting and socially marginalizing effects of identifying God exclusively with maleness:

> Come be our mother we are your young ones
> Come be our bride we are your lover
> Come be our dwelling we are your inhabitants....
> Come be our victory we are your army
> Come be our laughter we are your story
> Come be our Shekhinah we are your glory
> We believe that you live
> though you delay we believe you will certainly come....
>
> When the transformation happens as it must
> When we remember
> When she wakes from her long repose in us
> When she wipes the nightmare

of history from her eyes
When she returns from exile
When she utters her voice in the streets
In the opening of the gates . . .
When she crosses the land
Shaking her breasts and hips
With timbrels and with dances. . . . [54]

By treating the Shekhinah and her divine femaleness as a living part of Jewish religious tradition, the designs of this poem go beyond *poesis*. Its language is meant not just as poetry but as prayer, summoning the Shekhinah to action, and summoning readers to identify themselves with a religious community in which she is recognized as a vital form of divinity. In contrast to the patriarchal tradition that so often treats the female body with suspicion, disdain and disgust, this poem treats it as a revelation of divine presence; by imagining a Shekhinah who will be as compassionate as a mother, as committed to intimacy as a bride, the poem affirms the spiritual value of women's lives. As the title's indefinite article makes clear, the poem is also intended to be exemplary, to show how easy it would be re-gender patriarchal tradition, to make femaleness the default mode of conceiving divinity and write liturgy strewn with "She"s rather than "He"s.

But as radical as this glimpse of Shekhinah-centered worship is, in some ways, the Shekhinah invoked by this poem still reflects patriarchal tradition. Though the speakers of the poem imagine that in the future, the Shekhinah will wield a world- and history-changing power comparable to that of the Biblical God, in the here-and-now of the poem's invocation, she, like the Shekhinah of tradition, is passive, hidden, locked away in a future the speakers are sure will come but which neither they nor the Shekhinah have yet brought about. And like the traditional Shekhinah, Ostriker's Shekhinah is spoken of and to rather than speaking for herself. It is Ostriker and the speakers, not the Shekhinah, who recenter patriarchal tradition and regender its sacred language. The Shekhinah herself remains silent and still, a Sleeping Beauty whom the speakers of the poem call on but do not awaken.

As this critique suggests, even feminist evocations of the Shekhinah may be read as inadvertently extending patriarchal assumptions. That is why, even as some Jewish feminists were working to give the Shekhinah a larger role in Jewish religious and cultural practice, others, like Marcia Falk, were arguing that these efforts were self-defeating, because the Shekhinah is bound to reflect the patriarchal ideas of the tradition from which she emerged:

> I cannot help but feel that, far from redeeming women, the image of the Shekhinah has, until now, only supported the male-centered vision. In Jewish tradition, the Shekhinah has never been on equal footing with the mighty *Kadosh Barukh Hu*, 'the Holy-One-Blessed-Be-He,' her creator, her master, her groom, the ultimate reality of which she was only a manifestation. And while I like the name itself— Shekhinah, from the Hebrew root meaning "I dwell"— I would like to see in-dwelling, or immanence, portrayed in ways that are not secondary to transcendence. So too I would like to see autonomous female images, not ones that imply the essential otherness of women. (42–43)[55]

As Falk points out, tradition defines the Shekhinah's divine femaleness not only in opposition but subordination to God's divine maleness. God is in the heavens; the Shekhinah is on earth. God acts; the Shekhinah is passive. God sends Israel into exile; the Shekhinah goes with them. God splits seas, thunders, overthrows and lifts up nations, rules history but is not subject to it; the Shekhinah suffers with the human beings she dwells among. God thunders, decrees, instructs, comforts, foretells, talks and talks and talks; the Shekhinah holds her tongue.

Ostriker's poem pushes against the traditional Shekhinah's gender-binary limitations not only by making her the center of liturgical attention, but by identifying her in ways that are not gendered at all, as when "we" call her to be "our dwelling," "our victory," and so on. However, the Shekhinah's passivity and silence in the poem show why Falk is skeptical of efforts to use the Shekhinah as an antidote to patriarchy. Unlike the male-identified God we see in Jewish tradition, the Shekhinah in this poem doesn't make her own choices, express her own views, identify herself in her own terms (she doesn't even get to say "I am"), or, in the present, demonstrate her power and presence—and as a result, she inadvertently reflects traditional, patriarchal ideas.

Shekhinah Speaks comes late to feminist arguments over the Shekhinah—so late that the Shekhinah is no longer a bone of contention, freeing me to embrace her contradictions without taking sides or trying to resolve them.[56] *Shekhinah Speaks* follows Ostriker's poem and rabbinic tradition in identifying the Shekhinah in ways that are traditionally gendered female; it follows Ostriker in also identifying her in non-gendered ways as well. But unlike Ostriker's Shekhinah, who remains silent as she is identified by others, these poems aim to present an "autonomous female" Shekhinah by, among other things, letting the Shekhinah identify herself:

> I married you young,
> before you were conceived,
> waiting inside you like a frozen egg,
>
> building your foundations,
> crowning your head....
>
> I stretch out your curtains, strengthen your pegs,
> make room inside you for the world
> I created you to share. You
>
> are my embryo and I am your womb;
> you are my labor pains
> and I'm the mother pushing you
>
> to cry, to talk, to stand for something,
> to stop being ashamed
> of the joy you feel
>
> rising like waters in the days of Noah ...
> (from "Sing Out O Barren One")[57]

Though the Shekhinah here embraces roles, such as mother, and qualities, such as unconditional love, that are traditionally gendered female, her femaleness is not defined in opposition or subordination to maleness. Like male versions of divinity, she presents herself as active, articulate, and powerful, as well as in terms, like "frozen egg," that don't fit gender categories at all.

Though my reasons are different, like Falk, I want the Shekhinah to model what it might mean to be autonomously female. I grew up with the idea that gender transition meant changing myself to fit binary ideas of what it means to be a woman; when I finally embarked on that process, I thought that I had to act in conventionally feminine ways to show that my female gender identification was real. But the longer I lived as a woman, the clearer it became that I would never be female in the way the gender binary defines it. I had been born male, socialized as a male, had fathered children, published and taught as a male. The only way I can be female is in an autonomous sense, female in a way that is independent of binary definitions and so can include the aspects of my life that were shaped by or bound up with maleness.

The Shekhinah who speaks in these poems has never been defined by binary gender categories, has never concealed or amputated or denied aspects of herself to fit human ideas of femaleness. Her voice shows me what it sounds like to embrace, without shame or apology, a female identity untethered to biology and unimaginable in terms of the gender binary.

Of course, the Shekhinah is not a perfect role model. As a divine being, the Shekhinah doesn't waste a moment worrying about her gender identity or expression, any more than the God we see in the Bible wastes a moment worrying whether this or that behavior, word choice or tone of voice would be considered masculine. But if the Shekhinah doesn't care about fitting human ideas of gender, why bother to identify as female?

Gender categories are not very good at defining what human and divine beings *are*, but they can help us define our relationships with one another. Gender, among many other things, is a language of kinship, belonging, connection. It may make theological sense to refer to God as a genderless "It," but many religious people, including me, would feel alienated if we did so. Though contemporary liturgies often address divinity in gender-neutral terms such as "parent" that don't have the objectifying impact of "It," as every poet knows, such words are more abstract than their gendered equivalents. Stripped of the connotations of shared experience, of the joy and suffering and longing that freight our "mothers" and "fathers," "shes" and "hes," such terms can't conjure the same sense of connection with divinity.

The Shekhinah identifies as female not because she *is* what human beings mean by female, but because presenting herself as female enables her to relate to us with an intimacy otherwise impossible for a disembodied being, an effect we see at the end of Rachel Adler's "Second Hymn to the Shekhinah":

> I am your daughter, Lady,
> And pregnant with you.[58]

The speaker's Escher-like relationship with the Shekhinah, in which each brings forth the other, is expressed in terms of the female identification they share, which enables them to relate to one another simultaneously as mothers and daughters. That is how the poetics of binary gender works: by associating femaleness (and, of course, maleness) with bodies, physical experiences, and social roles, even when the individuals we identify as female don't, like the Shekhinah, completely fit those associations. But the Shekhinah's divinity transfigures gender, freeing the roles of mother and daughter from time, causality, and biology, so that Adler's speaker can be born out of the female divinity, "the Lady," she herself is carrying in her womb.

For most of my life, I relied on the poetics of binary gender to maintain the illusion that, despite identifying as female, I really was the man others took me for. When I began my transition, I turned to those poetics for the opposite purpose: to express my sense of being female through clothing, gestures, and so on. But ironically, the poetics of binary gender told me nothing about how to write poetry as a woman. In an effort to learn to do so, I started writing poems composed solely of language sampled from women's magazines—language written by, for, and about women.

Shekhinah Speaks has challenged me to learn a different kind of poetics, a poetics of divinity, ways of using language that signify divine voice and presence. I approached learning these poetics the way I approached learning to write as a woman: by composing poems from language sampled from texts traditionally accepted as signifying divinity, in this case, language from God's monologues in Isaiah, which, unlike many other Biblical examples of divine speech, are also magnificent poetry:

> For a long time I have kept silent,
> I have been quiet and held myself back.
> But now, like a woman in childbirth,
> I cry out, I gasp and pant.
> I will lay waste the mountains and hills
> and dry up all their vegetation; I will turn rivers into islands
> and dry up the pools. I will lead the blind by ways they
>   have not known,
> along unfamiliar paths I will guide them;
> I will turn the darkness into light before them
> and make the rough places smooth. (Isaiah 42:14-16)

Each poem in *Shekhinah Speaks* is partly composed of diction like this, diction charged with divine authority. Isaiah's monologues offer more than evocative nouns and verbs, such as "childbirth," "pools," "gasp" and "waste," and suggestive phrases, like "turn the darkness" and "dry up all." They also model divine tone, manner, and rhetoric. Isaiah's God brags, consoles, threatens, promises and laments, often in the same utterance, a characteristic that is even more prominent in Biblical Hebrew, which is far less punctuated than English translations.

Such rapid shifts in mood and manner are often combined, as they are here, with a torrent of first-person declarations through which God explicitly identifies in multiple, often contradictory ways: as someone who "kept silent" and someone who "cries out"; as being "like a woman in childbirth," an image of suffering and vulnerability; as a disembodied force who devastates the landscape; and, in another turn, as a tender caregiver who guides those who can't see.

These shifting self-identifications produce a kind of cognitive over-load, telling us too much too fast to make any stable sense of God. This is the most important thing Isaiah has taught me about the poetics of divinity. By implicitly and explicitly identifying in multiple ways, so that any glimpse of divinity a given phrase offers is complicated by the phrases that follow, God shows that God can never be more than momentarily understood in human terms. But even as they show that God doesn't fit into identity-defining categories, God's use of these inadequate terms also shows God's determination to be known, however provisionally, by the human beings God addresses, to be recognized as a living presence in the human world of irrigation and vegetation and childbirth that reveals the divinity it cannot contain.

But Isaiah's poetics of divinity always emphasize God's transcendence: though God comes close to human lives (close enough to guide the blind), God never identifies in ways that suggest God understands what human circumstances such as blindness or drought or earthquake feel like to human beings. Isaiah's God may cry out *like* a woman in childbirth, but we are never given to think that God shares the pain of labor.

Unlike Isaiah's God, the Shekhinah identifies herself in ways that show not only her transcendence of human categories but her immanence, her intimate engagement with and understanding of the human "you" she addresses. Immanence is one of the Shekhinah's defining traits (as Falk notes, her name derives from the Hebrew word "to dwell"), and that trait is traditionally understood as the female counterpart—complementary but also, as Falk says, "secondary"—to the male-identified God's transcendence. But as we see in Adler's hymn, the Shekhinah's immanence isn't secondary to transcendence; it is a form of transcendence. The Shekhinah is no more bound by human time and space than Isaiah's God; borne within those she bears, conceiving those who conceive her, she comprehends humanity inside and out.

The Shekhinah's binary-defying combination of immanence and transcendence has less in common with Isaiah's poetics of divinity than with those of Walt Whitman who, in "Song of Myself," also presents a speaker who demonstrates both his transcendence of human categories and his intimate engagement with them:

I am of old and young, of the foolish as much as the wise,
Regardless of others, ever regardful of others,
Maternal as well as paternal, a child as well as a man,
Stuffed with the stuff that is coarse, and stuffed with the
    stuff that is fine . . .
A southerner soon as a northerner, a planter nonchalant
    and hospitable,
A Yankee bound my own way . . . ready for trade . . . [59]

Like Isaiah's God, Whitman's speaker demonstrates his transcendence by identifying himself in shifting and often contradictory terms. A speaker who can be "A southerner as soon as a northerner" clearly transcends both categories. But unlike those of Isaiah's God, these self-identifications also show that while he is not *only* a southerner or a northerner, old or young, maternal or paternal, he identifies with and shares the ways of being these terms name. Even when Whitman's speaker comes close to transcending human circumstance completely, as when he says, "I pass death with the dying, and birth with the new-washed babe. . . . and am not / contained between my hat and boots," he always includes signs of his immanence, as he does when he reminds us that though he transcends birth and death, he still wears "hat and boots."[60] Like the Shekhinah's, the transcendence Whitman's speaker demonstrates through his shifting self-definitions is inseparable from his immanence: they identify him so closely with the humanity he addresses that at one point he declares that "It is you talking just as much as myself. . . . I act as the tongue of you."[61]

Whitman's speaker demonstrates his combination of transcendence and immanence by identifying himself with and through contradictory human categories, a form of the poetics of divinity that paradoxically affirms the humanity he shares with the "you" he addresses. Though the Shekhinah is divine rather than human, she, like Whitman's speaker, wants us to hear her speaking not only *to* us but *in* us, as though she is the tongue of us, identifying us in ways that summon us to become what she, who created us, knows we are meant to be. But no matter how intimate the Shekhinah is with humanity, she is not one of us: she is as different from the humanity to whom she speaks as a womb is from the embryo it surrounds and sustains.

This difference means that the Shekhinah requires a different poetics of divinity than that of Whitman's speaker. Though she too identifies herself in terms of multiple, conflicting categories, throughout *Shekhinah Speaks*, she spends much more time identifying herself by demonstrating her understanding of "you," naming "you" in multiple ways and from multiple perspectives, a barrage of shifting identifications that summon us to recognize that we, like her, overflow the terms that seem to define us:

> ...You
>
> are a vigil I keep;
> a flock I pasture;
> a grape on the vine
>
> still bursting with blessing
> even at the end of harvest,
> and I'm the light
>
> you're afraid of losing,
> the light revealing
> what it means to be human.
>
> Not an indecipherable mess; not a pot
> of meat and feeling,
> or a headstone covered with body paint,
>
> or a burning garden, or irony sweating.
> A new song
> you and I are singing,
>
> me through you and you through me,
> about the earth and heaven
> and the love
>
> you and I are making. (from "Revelation")[62]

Here and elsewhere, the Shekhinah insists that we can only recognize our kinship with her by expanding our understanding of our own humanity. But for me, it's easier to identify with the non-human Shekhinah than to see myself as part of humanity. That's the way I grew up, believing that my inability to fit binary gender categories in a world where everyone had to be simply male or female meant I wasn't human. Perhaps that is why, when I read "Song of Myself," the speaker's innumerable self-identifications don't convince me that I am included in either the "you" he addresses or the vast self he proclaims. Nowadays, I admire more than ever Whitman's effort to use poetry to hold his soon-to-be-dis-United States together by showing his readers that those we see as categorically different are, in fact, integral to our multitude-containing selves. But like many others readers, I am not ready to allow Whitman's speaker to act as the tongue of me.

When the Shekhinah addresses "you," she doesn't claim to identify with each and every kind of person, nor does she to try convince us to do so. She simply ignores the distinctions human beings make between one another. Black people and white people, heteronormative and queer, progressive and conservative, immigrant and native, disabled and able-bodied, believer and atheist—no matter how different we seem to one another, to the Shekhinah, all human beings are comprehended by the same second-person pronoun.

For me, that is the hardest part of the Shekhinah's poetics of divinity, the part that makes me want to close my ears and run away, and, by unsettling me so profoundly, convinces me of her divinity: her demand that I recognize in myself the humanity she sees, and summons each of us to see, as her offspring and her dwelling place. As love she is revealing.

NOTES

Introduction

1 I detail my experiences of coming out at Yeshiva University in my memoir of gender transition, *Through the Door of Life: A Jewish Journey Between Genders*, University of Wisconsin Press, 2012.

I: TRANS AND OTHER WAYS OF BEING HUMAN

Once Out of Nature: Reflections on Body, Soul, Gender and God

2 These days, transsexuals are recognized as one among many groups gathered within the category "transgender," an umbrella term that includes relations to gender and identity more complicated than the "natural" binary of male and female. For a more detailed explanation of the terms I use, see "A Note on Terminology."

3 Germaine Greer. "Caster Semenya Sex Row: What Makes a Woman?" *The Guardian.* August 20, 2009.

4 I explore the theological implications of this analogy between transgender and divine difficulty fitting human categories at length in the Introduction and chapters 1 and 3 of *The Soul of the Stranger: Reading God and Torah from a Transgender Perspective.*

What We Talk About When We Talk About Gender Dysphoria: An Address to Psychotherapists

5 A shorter version of this essay appeared online as "Disordering Gender: Breaking the Transgender Taboo" in *Psychology Tomorrow* in 2015.

6 Talia Bettcher has written extensively about the tendency to characterize transgender people, particularly transsexuals, as "deceivers," and about the psychological and physical violence to which these characterizations can lead.

We Pass for What We Are: Otherness and Humanness

7 Developed from a lecture given to The William Alanson White Psychoanalytic Society, March 12, 2021.

8 See J.-F. Staszak. (2009). "Other/Otherness." In Kitchin R. and Thrift N. (eds.), *International Encyclopaedia of Human Geography,* Oxford: Elsevier, vol. 8: 43–47.

9 I discuss this formula, which is still central to the way many transsexuals

(those, like me, assigned to one binary gender at birth but strongly identifying with the other) understand themselves and are understood by therapists
and others who support their transitions, and is still used as a rhetorical tool
in the increasingly bitter political battles over trans and non-binary rights and
treatment, at length in "What We Talk About When We Talk About Gender
Dysphoria: An Address to Psychotherapists."

10 Du Bois, W.E.B. *The Soul's of Black Folk*. Ed. Brent Hayes Edwards. Oxford
World's Classics. Oxford UP, 2007. 8.

11 Emerson, Ralph Waldo. "Self-Reliance." In *Essays*. Ed. Edna H.L. Turpin.
Project Gutenberg E-Book. 2005. 90.

Anachronism is always hard to avoid when quoting statements written in
different historical eras, particularly when, as is so often the case with Emerson,
it is hard to pin down the original meaning even in context. The phrase "We pass
for what we are" appears in the context of an argument (if one can use that term
for such allusive, associative assertions) whose thrust is that no matter how we
may try to disguise it, we cannot stop living in ways that express who we really
are—or, as Emerson puts it, our "nature" or "character." The person we try to
present ourselves as being is always shadowed, and ultimately overshadowed,
by what Emerson sees as our essential "greatness." But this simultaneously chas-
tening and comforting thought is preceded by an extended rant criticizing the
ways we blur, diminish, and betray the greatness Emerson sees as our true selves
by "conformity," i.e., clinging to social conventions and identities that make us
intelligible, acceptable, and predictable to others. So though Emerson certainly
does not mean "we pass" in the contemporary sense of concealing LGBTQ identities, he does seem to mean that those who conform to social conventions and
fit identities that go with them are "passing" as other and less than who we are, a
reading reinforced by the model "coming out" script he offers to those who are
ready to stop conforming and "live in truth," a script whose language eerily antic-
ipates that of contemporary LGBTQ coming out statements. This is not because
Emerson is concerned with (or even aware of) non-heteronomative forms of
identity, but because he shares with contemporary LGBTQ+ people an awareness that our fears of violating social norms lead many of us—Emerson would
say almost all of us—to closet our truths, our nature, our character, our sense of
who we really are.

12 There are many different reasons we may feel that we are passing as or pretending to be who we are supposed to be. Some, like imposter syndrome, are
situational, reflecting anxieties about our about ability to fulfill some role or
task, or our efforts to conceal something about ourselves. The variation I call
"internalized otherness" is not specific to any situation or or aspect of ourselves.
It is awareness that no matter where or who we are, we don't completely fit the
terms and roles that define us in relation to others, and on which we rely to
define ourselves.

13 I develop this idea from a trans theological perspective in chapter 5 of *The Soul
of the Stranger: Reading God and Torah from a Transgender Perspective*. HBI
Series on Jewish Women. Brandeis UP, 2018.

II: TRANS AND OTHER WOMEN

"I am She as You are She as You are Me and We are All Together": The Politics of Identifying as a Woman

14 While there are also conflicts between anti-trans feminists and nonbinary people, trans men, and those who embrace other forms of trans identity, the longest
running conflict is with trans women, also called male-to-female transsexuals,
who identify as women. That is the conflict I can speak to personally, and is the
focus of this essay.

15 We see the same problems cropping up wherever we find identity politics, including within what is called "the transgender community." For example, some transsexuals feel they have little in common with those who have non-binary gender
identities and resent being lumped into the same "we," and some who identify as
nonbinary criticize transsexuals for perpetuating binary gender oppression. The
term "transgender" includes so many relationships to gender that when I say "I
am transgender," I hardly feel I am constituting any identity at all.

16 This quote was taken from the website in April 2015; the school's policy has and
likely will continue to change.

Diving into the Wreck: Trans and Anti-Trans Feminism

17 Like the previous essay, this one focuses on conflicts over the meaning of
"woman," and thus the inclusion or exclusion of trans women, also called male-
to-female transsexuals, who identify as women. This focus is not meant to erase
or diminish the conflicts between anti-trans feminists and nonbinary people,
trans men, and those who embrace other forms of trans identity. But the longest
running conflict, and the one I have been part of, is with trans women, and,
though my arguments, I believe, apply equally to other forms of transgender
and nonbinary identity, that is the focus of this essay.

18 Koyama, Emi. 2003. "Transfeminist Manifesto." In *Catching a Wave: Reclaiming
Feminism for the 21st Century*. 244–259. Boston: Northeastern UP, 2003. 245.

19 Burkett, Elinor. 2015. "What Makes a Woman?" *The New York Times*. June 6,
2015.

20 Rich, Adrienne. *Diving into the Wreck: Poems, 1971–1972*. NY: W.W. Norton,
1972. 23–24.

21 Raymond, Janice. *The Transsexual Empire: The Making of the She-Male*. Athene
Series. Teachers College Press, 1994.

22 Bettcher, Talia. 2015. "Intersexuality, Transgender, and Transsexuality." In *The
Oxford Handbook of Feminist Theory*. Ed. Lisa Disch and Mary Hawkesworth.
Oxford: Oxford UP. Oxford Handbooks Online.

23 Ibid, 4–5.

24 Ibid, 9.

25 Hirsh, Elizabeth. 1994. "Another Look at Genre: Diving into the Wreck of Ethics
with Rich and Irigaray." In *Feminist Measures: Soundings in Poetry and Theory*.
Ed. Lynn Keller and Cristanne Miller. 117–138. Ann Arbor: U. of Michigan
Press. 118.

26 *Diving into the Wreck*, 3.

27 Ibid, 24.

28 As Bettcher and others have pointed out, Rich's use of the androgyne as a metaphor or sign of a theoretical relation to gender is often seen in discussion of
trans figures in queer theory.

29 Hirsch, 135.

30 Boylan, Jennifer Finney. 2012. "'What Kind of Times are These?': On Adrienne
Rich and Trans-Misogyny." Author's blog. April 18, 2012.

31 Butler, Judith. *Gender Trouble: Feminism and the Subversion of Identity.* NY:
Routledge, 1990. vii.

32 *Diving into the Wreck*, 19.

III: TRANS AND OTHER ACTS OF SELF CREATION

Ours for the Making: Trans Lit, Trans Poetics

33 In the decade-plus since this essay was published in 2011, there has been sig-
nificant progress in terms of trans literature: Amazon (of course) has lists of
best-selling trans-related books in various genres, the Lambda Literary Awards
now have separate awards for poetry, fiction, and non-fiction (though the latter
category, in particular, lumps widely different kinds of writing together), some
universities have offered trans-specific literature classes, and there has been a
trickle of memoirs describing more kinds of trans identities and lives, including
the lives of trans people of color. There are also some small presses that emphasize books by trans and nonbinary authors. But publishing opportunities,
reviews and other publicity, hiring of openly trans and nonbinary writers and
literature professors, and trans-lit-oriented classes are still few and far between.

34 My most extensive use of this technique was *The Book of Anna*, a novel-like
work written in the voice of a fictional woman, Anna, through whom I was
able to explore a female point of view without revealing my female gender
identification.

"Myself—the Term Between": A Trans Poetic Autobiography

35 Binary gender's insistence on physical sex as the basis of identity also leads to erasure—including non-consensual "corrective" genital surgeries—of people who
are intersex, whose physical sex cannot be categorized as male or female, and
whose existence contradicts the gender binary assumption that every human
being must be one or the other. In other words, binary gender isn't biological
realism, a simple recognition of the reality and importance of human bodies, as
both anti-trans feminists and conservatives often argue. Binary gender is an ideology, an idea about rather than factual description of humanity. This ideology
is so strong that doctors have often operated on intersex newborns, sometimes
without consulting or even informing their parents, to "correct" their genitalia by
making them appear either male or female.

36 Though "transsexual" has been joined by many more nouns referring to identities that don't fit binary gender, not only have these new nouns not solved the

basic problem, their rapid multiplication and lack of widely-agreed-upon definitions has in some ways made trans and nonbinary identities harder to express
and understand. The few widely used terms like "transgender" and "nonbinary"
are politically and socially useful shorthand, but they encompass too many different relationships between body, psyche, personal history and cultural categories to express or represent very much.

37 "Poetics" not only refers to poetry, but to the theory and practice of any form of
literary discourse.

38 I was an early voice in developing the concept of trans poetics, starting with my
"Trans Poetics Manifesto" and "Ours for the Making" (see above) and continu-
ing in "I am not not me: Unmaking and Remaking the Language of the Self,"
also published online by LambdaLiterary.org, and, some years later, a more academic essay, "Split It Open and Count the Seeds": Trans Identity, Trans Poetics,
and Oliver Bendorf's The Spectral Wilderness. *TSQ: Transgender Studies
Quarterly.* 3.3–4 (November 2016): 637–648.

39 Ladin, Jay. *Alternatives to History.* Riverdale, NY: Sheep Meadow Press, 67–89.

40 Ibid, 39.

41 In much of my post-transition writing, I've embraced this posture not as camouflage but as a commitment to revealing the ways understanding transgender
experience can illuminate and expand our understanding of what it means to be
human.

42 *Alternatives to History,* 46–54.

43 The first edition of *The Book of Anna* was published in 2007 by Sheep Meadow
Press under the name J. Ladin. A revised second edition, including an author's
afterward that tells the story of the book's origins and composition from a different perspective, was published by EOAGH Press and won the 2021 National
Jewish Book Award for Poetry.

44 There has been a lot of writing about the literary difficulties of representing the
Holocaust, but as far as I know, no one has yet looked at these difficulties from
a trans poetic perspective.

45 *The Book of Anna.* Second edition. Brooklyn, NY: EOAGH, 2021. 17.

46 James discusses world-formulas at length in *Pragmatism: A New Name for Some
Old Ways of Thinking,* though he speaks in terms of philosophies and psyches
rather than sentences (NY: Longman, Greens & Co., 1947).

47 American Psychiatric Association. *Diagnostic and Statistical Manual of Mental
Disorders, DSM-IV-TR.* 4th edition (text revision). American Psychiatric
Publishers. 2000.

48 Ladin, Joy. *Transmigration.* Riverdale, NY: Sheep Meadow Press, 2009. 23.

49 Ibid. 35–6.

50 Unpublished draft of "Half the Human Race," which appeared in very different
form in *The Future is Trying to Tell Us Something: New and Selected Poems,*
Rhinebeck, NY: Sheep Meadow Press, 110.

51 Bakhtin, *The Dialogic Imagination: Four Essays by M.M. Bakhtin,* ed. Michael
Holquist, trans. Caryl Emerson and Michael Holquist (Austin: U of Texas P,
1981).

52 Selinger, Eric. "Shekhinah in America." In *Jewish American Poetry: Poems, Commentary, Reflections.* Ed. Jonathan N. Barron and Eric Murphy Selinger. Hanover, NH: Brandeis UP, 2000. 251.

53 Ibid.

54 Ostriker, Alicia. *The Nakedness of the Fathers: Biblical Visions and Revisions.* New Brunswick, NJ: Rutgers UP, 1997. 253–254.

55 See Marcia Falk, "Notes on Composing New Blessings toward a Feminist-Jewish Reconstruction of Prayer," *Journal of Feminist Studies in Religion*, vol. 3 no. 1, Spring 1987, pp. 39–53.

56 Since this essay first appeared, "Shekhinah Speaks" has been completed and published by selva oscura (2022). When this essay quotes from these poems, it is referring to intermediate drafts that differ significantly from the book versions.

57 "Sing Out O Barren One" appeared in *Moment*, Spring 2019: 35. A substantially revised version, retitled "Singing," appears in *Shekhinah Speaks.*

58 Adler, Rachel. "Second Hymn to Shekhinah." *Response: A Contemporary Jewish Review* 13(1/2): 1982, 260.

59 Whitman, Walt. *Leaves of Grass.* 1855. 23. whitmanarchive.org/published/LG/1855/whole.html

60 Ibid, 17.

61 Ibid, 53.

62 Ladin, Joy. *Shekhinah Speaks.* Chicago, IL: selva oscura press, 2022. 16–17.